THE
ROYAL ROAD
OF LIFE

BEGINNING YOUR PATH
OF INNER PEACE, VIRTUE,
AND A LIFE OF PURPOSE

RYUHO
OKAWA

IRH Press

BOOKS
IRH PRESS
New York

ISBN 13: 978-1-942125-53-2
ISBN 10: 1-942125-53-4

Printed in Canada
First Edition

Cover Design: Whitney Cookman

TABLE OF
CONTENTS

Preface • 9

CHAPTER ONE

INTRODUCTION TO
THE ROYAL ROAD OF LIFE

1 Embarking on the Royal Road • 12
2 The Existence of the Other World • 17
3 The Journey on the Royal Road • 21
Abandoning Attachments
Having the Heart of Tolerance
Becoming One with Nature

CHAPTER TWO

SERENITY OF MIND

1 Moments of Inner Peace • 34
2 Feeling the Mystical • 38
3 What Happens When You Worry • 41
4 Ways to Maintain Peace of Mind • 45
Take Time for Silence
Do Not Get Angry
Cultivate a Tolerant Heart
Give Things Time
Apologize Sincerely

5 Like a Warm Autumn Day • 55

CHAPTER THREE

REBUILDING YOUR LIFE

1 Resentment Cannot Be Healed through Resentment • 60

2 The First Step: Stopping the Negative Thoughts
in Your Mind • 67

3 The Second Step: The Study of People • 74
Studying the Unhappy
Studying the Successful

4 The Third Step: The Cultivation of
Ideals and Passion • 83

5 The Fourfold Path and Rebuilding Your Life • 87

CHAPTER FOUR

LIVING IN ETERNITY NOW

1 Perceptions of Time • 90

2 Time That Generates Value • 95

3 Inventions and Investments to Increase Time • 100

4 Increasing the Density of Time • 106

5 Increasing the Area of Time • 111

6 The Volume of Time, the Sum Total of a Life • 115

7 Budgeting Time: Turning Time into Gold • 116

CHAPTER FIVE

THE PATH TO HUMAN COMPLETION

1 A Journey of Eternal Hopes and Ideals • 124

2 The Burning Desire of Your Soul • 127

3 Your Guardian Spirit Is Standing Beside You • 130

4 The Achievement Is Not Mine Alone • 132

5 The Great Tree of Life • 136

6 The Path to Human Completion • 139
Awakening to Your True Mission
Freeing the Potential Within You
Accumulating Wisdom
The Exploration of the Right Mind

CHAPTER SIX

ON THE ROYAL ROAD OF LIFE

1 The True Leader • 154

2 Respect, the First Condition of a True Leader • 156

3 Wisdom, the Second Condition of a True Leader • 161

4 Belief, the Third Condition of a True Leader • 163

5 Righteousness, the Fourth Condition of
a True Leader • 166

6 Courage, the Fifth Condition of a True Leader • 169

7 Self-Reflection on the Five Virtues of Leadership • 171

8 Love, the Foundation of All Five Virtues • 174

9 On the Royal Road of Life • 177

CHAPTER SEVEN

THE AGE OF DAYBREAK

A SPECIAL LECTURE AT THE UNIVERSITY OF TOKYO

1 From Taking Love from Others to Giving Love • 184

2 Cultivate Your Roots • 187

The Path to Becoming a Cultivated Person
The Path to Becoming a Thinker

3 Think Strategically • 192

4 Take Care of Yourself Physically • 195

5 Signs of a New Era • 197

6 The Roots of Democracy • 199

7 The Age of the Sun • 206

Afterword • 209

About the Author • 213

About Happy Science • 216

About IRH Press USA • 220

Books by Ryuho Okawa • 221

Preface

The royal road of life is your path to true success. In this book, I explain the secrets for maturing into a leader by starting with controlling your mind. Everyone acknowledges that the mind exists, but there are great differences to the depths we understand it.

Some of you picture the mind as your emotions, while others imagine it simply as brain functions. The depth of your understanding of the word "mind" is what I believe determines the capacity of your life. If you have looked into your mind deeply and grasped its true nature, you will see that these pages contain concrete truths, not just abstract ideas.

To find success in the true meaning, you have to seek it while correcting and elevating your mind. The royal road of life is your path to a true happiness that continues from this world to the other world.

Ryuho Okawa
*President** *
Happy Science
March 1993

---

* His current title is Master and CEO of Happy Science Group.

CHAPTER ONE

INTRODUCTION TO THE ROYAL ROAD OF LIFE

1
EMBARKING ON THE ROYAL ROAD

Have you been aware of your mind itself over the course of your life? That we all have a mind is something you have surely known, but looking within your mind is something perhaps very few of you have done. The royal road of life begins, at first, with getting an understanding of your mind. As you notice various changes arise in your surroundings, whether they are occurrences, events, or the words spoken by many kinds of people, you invariably react to them unconsciously. There is always some way you respond to them, and the shape that these responses take is your inner emotions.

Perhaps talking about emotions will make a lot of sense to you. The most well-known of them are joy, anger, sorrow, and pleasure, and we had been endowed with these feelings to some extent even before we were taught about them. Without having to learn how, we have been expressing these emotions since the time of our birth, and the emotions we now experience as adults probably developed based on them.

Even if you have been aware of your emotions, however, I'm certain that you have felt frustrated about always responding with the same emotions to the same pattern of circumstances. Some people are quick to anger and cannot hold back from lashing out in rage. They get upset about acting this way and keep wondering why this happens, but they cannot rid these emotions from themselves, so they remain at a loss, in a dismal state. Another emotion that people experience is sadness, and there are some people living in sadness every day who aren't able to understand why. Around them, there seems to be no one else in deeper sadness, and they live each day as if in a state of mourning. Life itself is sadness to them— there are some people who think in this way.

When you are at the peak of your joy, perhaps you suddenly come to realize the hurt feelings you unknowingly caused to those close to you. When joyfulness fills your every day, everything seems rosy, and you in fact neglect to think of others' feelings. Through your words or deeds you hurt them, all the while not noticing their facial expressions changing and their seething glare looking back at you. Within this experience is a path that leads you to unknowingly become an egotist.

The same holds true with feelings of pleasure. When you become immersed in the delight of your work or the pursuit of your interests, it is easy for fairly many people to slip off the right course and fall prey to the charm of a life of pleasure. Before you know it, the ideals of your youth become long forgotten, and pleasure becomes the purpose of your life. You tell yourself that there is nothing wrong with chasing pleasures as long as they reward you with self-gratification, and your days begin naturally falling into this way of life. Before you realize it, the true purpose of human life is long forgotten from your mind.

Then, at the close of a lifetime of pleasure-seeking, death arrives. Though you believed that death would be the end of your existence, as well as those of others and the world around you, you shed your physical body and return to the other world. Once you are there, you are faced with a hard truth awaiting you. Those who spent their lives indulging in pleasures are faced sternly with the truth that life continues after death, and they find themselves at an utter loss for words to express themselves. They are the people who had once laughed at and made a mockery of those who worked diligently and found their purpose in life in loving others.

Some people scorn and criticize others who are pursuing their ideals and living for the sake of others, accusing them of a poor outlook on life, insisting that life is much too brief not to indulge in pleasures. After departing from this world, these people will gradually realize that life's pleasures do, indeed, come at a high price. They will look back on their lives with profound regret, and from deep within their hearts will arise remorseful thoughts, saying, "If only I had known about this truth of our lives...If only I could turn back time and start my life over again. I ought to have devoted my life to something more precious. I went to the end of my life obsessed with gratifying my physical pleasures. What altogether a false life I led!" What could have caused these people to make this mistake?

The cause of this mistake lies in the views we hold about our human lives. Our lives have been something granted to us. Our success or failure at realizing this will make a big difference in our own life down the line. The view that our life is not something we received from God but something that belongs to us, not something our parents gave us but a result of coincidence, that we can spend our life however we wish because this is our life—this view can lead us to stray far away from the life we should be truly leading. It is simply that.

People of this modern age even fail to believe that our lives have been given to us; this is what modern people have become. Around the world, in the countries that are known to be developed nations, many people indeed are living in pursuit of their self-interest, assuming that there is nothing wrong about using their lives to fulfill their desires.

What could this way of thinking be producing? What could be spreading within the minds of such people? The medical treatment of cancer has advanced more and more, owing to the progress achieved in modern medicine. But there are people, in far too large a number, who remain unaware that cancerous cells are spreading within their minds, and when I see this, I fail to hold back my tears. The starting point of their way of thinking is wrong.

The physical bodies in which we all dwell are just the vessels, the automobiles. In your actual life, no matter how dearly you cherish the automobile you own, you would never mistake it for being yourself. Even if someone breaks your automobile down, or sells it, you would never think of it as yourself.

Unfortunately, however, a great part of people in the course of their lives believes that their physical bodies are themselves. Therefore, at the starting point on the royal road, you must turn around this belief completely and realize that the soul in your body is the main actor of your life.

2

THE EXISTENCE OF
THE OTHER WORLD

My intention is not to define the royal road for only the several decades we live in this world. There are already plenty of success philosophies out there in this world. By contrast, we at Happy Science seek a happiness that continues on from this world to the other world. Some readers may want to ask me, then, "How are we to think about that when we know nothing about the other world? Since all we know with certainty is this physical world, isn't seeking to be successful in this world enough?" But a truth is essentially singular; truths could never be 80 percent of the way true, 60 percent of the way true, or just halfway true. In the world of probability, there is a fifty-fifty probability that the other world exists, but in the world of reality, its existence has to either be 100 percent true or zero percent true. No other answer can exist.

The solemn truth is that no one has ever succeeded in disproving the other world's existence. A vast number of people in this age profess themselves to be atheists and say that they cannot believe in religion, or deny that the other world exists. But no one has ever succeeded in proving that they are right, as far as I am able to know. For a large majority of them, their wish to disbelieve is based on very personal feelings. They don't truly disbelieve in the other world's existence; they just want to deny it. They are afraid to think about it, so they refuse to give it any acknowledgement.

No one in the past has ever completely proved that the other world doesn't exist. By contrast, over the course of human history, there have been countless people who lived to prove that the other world exists. It is no exaggeration to say that every religious leader who ever lived had lived in devotion to this cause. And throughout the history of this world, in every age, there was always the presence of a religious leader who never stopped teaching about the world of God, the world beyond, and the existence of souls.

Each leader proved such existences in various ways. To make the existence of the other world and God known to others, there have been those, such as Jesus Christ and Moses, who performed miracles. Still, today, incurable illnesses are sometimes miraculously healed. Other than only these physical proofs, there were also many other leaders who continuously appeared, one after another, to expound teachings while receiving direct guidance from the invisible world. There were different ways that they accomplished this. Some used automatic writing to receive their teachings as words written down while their hands moved involuntarily. Other teachings were received through spiritual revelations, such as those of

Mohammad, who received his teachings from Allah while he cloistered himself in a cave. Yet others have channeled spiritual messages, which we also have many of at Happy Science, to show proof of the existence of the other world.

There are aspects of all these ways that have fallen short of persuading every person, of course, because of the difference between this world and the other world. These worlds would need to resemble each other exactly to find perfect evidence. We can make people see, touch, and examine things in this world, so they can confirm the things that exist here. But we cannot show them perfectly anything that exists in the other world. Even though there are many methods of proving it, we cannot do so because it is a world of a different dimension.

For this reason, God conceived of a method. He dispatched great saints to this world on Earth, again and again, to convey His words, perform miracles, and let many people experience other-worldly existences. Through these saints, God showed the people how to live as God would. People's reverence for these saints enabled them to imagine Him and the world of His creation.

I have just used the word, "imagine," but it could be replaced by "feel." Why are we able to feel the world of His creation? Because the act of belief exists in us. To *believe in* things which you can actually see and touch is not possible, you can only *confirm* their existence. But things that are invisible require a heart of belief, and when you're able to believe in them, you become transformed from a being of this earthly world to another-worldly being. When we human beings realize the existence of the higher, heavenly world, we become released from the material way of life we may have been attached to. That is why the act of believing holds such great meaning.

3

The Journey on the Royal Road

Abandoning Attachments

You have now been made aware of the world beyond this world. Now you will need to do some essential things as you make your way along life's royal road. The first is to abandon attachments.

This word, "attachment," can be explained in this simple way: While you go about your daily life, there are moments when you're lost in thought about a certain thing and then suddenly realize that you happened to be thinking about it. Attachments are these thoughts that constantly repeat in your mind in your daily life.

Your thoughts are difficult to deeply perceive unless you have explored your mind enough. But you might understand what attachments are and recognize them easily when I tell you that they are the recurring thoughts in your mind. For example, there are the mistakes you made in the past. If you've experienced failure at work, your mind may always be recalling this memory and making you break into a cold sweat. Or if you did poorly on your college entrance exam, perhaps that's all you're able to remember, as if it just happened yesterday. Or perhaps your mistake is marriage related and this memory feels as real as though it were yesterday or, in fact, as if it were happening now all over again. Also, your attachments do not come only from your past mistakes. They are also found in the present, in work-related matters, if your thoughts constantly dwell on them no matter what you do.

Of course, some exceptions exist. The thoughts you dwell on are sometimes exceedingly close to your ideals. When the inner compass needle of your "attachments" is pointing to a single place in Heaven, the place of God, then those thoughts should be truly considered "ideals." It would be unsuitable to call them "attachments." Of course, ideals may sometimes turn into attachments when mistaken ways are taken or misguided methods are used; this occurs very frequently. But a mind pointing to God is not an attachment but, in truth, is representing your ideal.

On the compass of the mind, however, the direction pointing to God is very narrow, and your mind's needle ordinarily is pointing to another one of the 360 degrees. You will realize that sometimes your compass is pointing to the direction of self-harm, at the world of sorrow and suffering. Other times, your mind may be directed toward other people, with dark thoughts regarding the pain and sorrow you want to bring them. This is typically the shape of an attachment.

If you do not yet fully understand the nature of the mind, you might not clearly understand the reason attachments are harmful, so let me explain. To the spiritual eye, your soul originally shines brightly, as brilliantly as diamonds and pure gold. When you first came into this world, this pure state was your soul. When I refer to your "soul," I mean the spiritual energy that is dwelling within your physical body and appears in the same shape. And when I refer to your "mind," I mean the central core of your soul, which governs your whole soul. As I said before, the soul was in a shining state in the beginning. It's likely that this isn't too difficult for you to believe; when you watch small children, you can easily recognize that this must have been very true. Because of their purity and innocence, they appear to be shining even to you, as you live in this material world. This is also the essential nature of your soul.

While growing up, however, debris and dust gradually gathered over your golden soul as a result of various kinds of setbacks, failures, and sorrows. Although you didn't notice it happening, debris and dust gradually accumulated. So you must begin by realizing that this soiled state is not truly your nature. Originally, you were not born in such a state. You must realize that the accumulated debris and dust are your attachments, whereas you, by nature, shine luminously. The world where we originally lived before birth was a place of purity and innocence where everyone loved one another and shared their happiness together, just as in the world of children.

As you grow into adulthood, however, disappointments and sorrows change the way you view other people, and your trust in them weakens without your even realizing it. The world appears as if it were harming you. Mistakes become countless, and sorrows grow endless. Absorbed deeply in those realities, you may doubt that what I'm about to say is true, but through the magnetic attraction within you, you draw these debris- and dust-like things to yourself, and eventually they accumulate. This is the reality. Innumerable people unknowingly live with thoughts of self-harm that are inviting harmful situations to themselves. When we look closely at this world, we see that it is full of people who love failure, unhappiness, and illness. They don't understand how to control the pointer of their mind, so they fix it in the direction of darkness and attract things that cover up their inner, golden light unknowingly. The inner light in them has become covered and dimmed and is now glowing with a shadowy light of gray.

My advice to you is not too difficult. If you can discover the truth of my words so far, resolving to become free of your attachment will be your first step toward happiness. In your mind, please think, "This has been true; thinking back, I see that my mind has always been pinned down to negative thoughts. Let me pull the nails out so my mind can be free." When you pull this nail out, you may still notice that it isn't enough to free your mind. So you will search for another nail pinning down your thoughts, and when you find it, you will also remove that one.

"Even if I have made mistakes at work, has it in any way lessened my worth? There are so many jobs in the world, and there are people striving to develop themselves while working within them and confronting difficulties. Considering that, isn't it fainthearted of me to always be dwelling on small failures in my past and blaming other people for them? Isn't it enough that I remove this nail myself? It's no one else's fault that I feel trapped by my mistakes. It's been my own doing, nailing myself down this way. There is nothing that can be done about what has already passed. But there has to be something I need to do; what could this something be? It must be to have a mind that is not attached to the unhappiness of your past. This must be the most important thing I am to do.

"When we look at the currents of a river, we sometimes see debris; bamboo scraps, fallen tree branches, fabric remnants, straw, and scraps of many kinds collect around wooden stakes standing in the river. This must be what the current state of our mind is like. We are the torpid waters around this wooden stake alongside the riverbank. But a river, by its nature, is meant to flow. A river, by essence, flows."

You must free yourself from attachments. To do so, you must part company with your past. At the same time, the only way to make use of your past is transforming it into precious lessons. You should not carry the past around with you unless you have turned it into precious lessons. The most important thing is to bid farewell to the unhappiness of your past, keep only the gems of lessons close to your heart, and live in the present.

In your heart there are all sorts of nails that have been driven in, one after another. Some may have been stuck there for ten or twenty years. To a spiritual eye, they have now become crooked and rusty. Why have you left them there, driven into your mind? You absolutely have to remove them. If you still suffer from the pain of a mistake you made twenty or thirty years ago, it isn't anyone's responsibility but your own.

The river's mission can only be fulfilled while it continues flowing. If it should ever become sluggish and stop, that will mean the end of its mission. For this reason, you have to become free of attachments. Therefore, the first thing you must do is realize this fact. After you have discovered this fact about yourself, the next thing you have to do is resolve in your will to free yourself. Hold this intention, and have this desire, because when you do, you will be able to remove the nails from your mind.

Having the Heart of Tolerance

As I have now explained, abandoning attachments is the most important thing to do on the royal road. Next in importance is cultivating a spirit, or heart, of tolerance. This virtue has long been lost from this world. How rarely we run into people with a tolerant heart these days. When I trace my memories, I find that such encounters have been very few. I wonder how many one year would bring me. How numerous are the people who no longer have a sense of this virtue. Before they could notice, their hearts have shrunk to such a degree that they overly keenly recognize slight flaws and find fault with others and themselves. Therefore, if your heart has now gained freedom from attachments, the next thing you will need is this heart, or spirit, of tolerance.

More than five billion people* are living on this Earth in various countries and under different circumstances. Some are starving; some are well-fed. Some are intellectual; some are not. Some are built with physical strength, some with physical feebleness. Some are dark-skinned, some are pale-skinned, and still others are yellow-skinned. Some have families; some are alone. In these ways, those five billion or more people are living in a wide range of situations and circumstances.

Imagine what this world must look like from the perspective of God. He must be thinking, "I accept this as good and that as also good. Whether someone is dark-skinned, pale-skinned, or yellow-skinned, I see them all as good. All people shall seek happiness from within their given environment. Therefore, you shall seek happiness from within your present circumstances." Our opinions vary, and we have complaints and dissatisfactions as people living on Earth, but how do the great eyes of God see us from the viewpoint of His great heart? For certain, He must be looking down compassionately on all of us, accepting all things as they are, because our lives are not

---

* The population of the world in 1990 when this lecture was given.

limited to this present one. Like the eternal river that begins from someplace and ends someplace that we cannot know, we have existed as souls since a time eternally long ago and have been born over and over again on Earth. At different times, we've been born in Africa, India, China, or Japan. Our souls have been reborn in various places. When we look at individual points in time, it is obvious to everyone that we are not always born into ideal circumstances. We have been born into many different environments under all kinds of conditions so that our long, nearly eternal life may become fruitful. Just as the stream runs down a mountain, forms a little valley, goes temporarily beneath leaves, becomes a brook that sometimes runs rapidly and at other times moves slowly, and eventually becomes a wide river flowing into the sea, our lives also form rapids, valleys, and pools to provide us with a variety of experiences in the eternal flow of reincarnation.

Having become aware of that fact, we should be much more tolerant toward ourselves, as well as other people. We cannot but have tolerance when we realize that each individual is living out his or her own unique time, going through soul-training that is part of the great flow. You must embrace yourself with kindness as well. When you come across a waterfall or a rapid in the long history of your soul, tell yourself, "You are giving your best effort. Although you may be going through a difficult time right now, this is just one point on a very long journey, so do not lose patience. The river will start to slow down eventually. Until then, do not get hasty, and instead, be tolerant of everything." This is an important attitude of heart to have.

Becoming One with Nature

The third important thing to do on the royal road of life is to keep your mind in harmony with nature. The main source of your present distress comes from judgments you have placed on yourself according to the standards of urban societies. Can you see how significantly city-based values have influenced your suffering? Some examples might be your need for a job at a company that's superior to others and the need to have a higher position than others on the corporate ladder, and, to achieve these, the need to get into a better college than others. More examples are the need for greater fame, status, and wealth than others; examples are so numerous that counting them up would be a never-ending task. And they all seem to stem from the values of urban society.

What we call urban values actually come from the stress of living a too busy life in an overcrowded, limited space. Because of that, we feel buried in the crowd, so we wish to win others' notice. This feeling could be your main source of hastiness and distress.

I ask you to look back over your life right now. You have been living through eternal time. What do you imagine your life would have been like if you had been born three hundred years ago? How about one thousand years ago? Next, imagine your life two thousand, then two thousand five hundred, then three thousand, five thousand, and finally ten thousand years ago. When you look back on such long-ago times, you may feel that this place you are living in now is not the true place for your soul to find happiness. Beyond this world on Earth, there is a world called Heaven, where the higher you ascend, the more calm and harmony prevail. In these worlds where the *bodhisattvas* and *tathagatas* live, there are no cities in sight. Those who live there are living in harmony with great nature. Existing within your mind is this familiar scenery of your soul. This world is the ideal world, the world of utopia, which dwells within you. Imagine yourself on a beautiful spring day, sitting beneath a cherry blossom tree on top of a hill, looking down on a misty landscape. A scene like this is within you. That is the scenic landscape that your soul longs for. On top of a hill of warm sunshine, beneath the cherry blossom tree and its beautiful birdsongs, you see blue mountains thinly veiled with mist in the far distance. This ideal world unfolding before your eyes represents the truth your heart longs for.

Many of us live in the hustle and bustle of a city, this is true. But let us still manifest the true shape of our souls and fulfill our hopes. To do so, please stop your busy thoughts and spend time each day or when there is enough time on the weekend to enjoy a calm and peaceful mind. In other words, please enjoy oneness with the great harmony of nature without intentions to do anything. This is the heavenly way of life for those who've started to learn the Truths; this is how we can begin walking the royal road that we should aim to traverse.

CHAPTER TWO

SERENITY

OF

MIND

1

Moments of Inner Peace

In this chapter, I would like to talk about the issues in the world of the mind that are faced by everyone. That is to say, as we each live our lives, there is much we are given to learn about, and I would like to talk about the kind of issues each of us shoulders, and how we should live our lives from this day on. These are the fundamental topics regarding our lives that will be covered in this chapter.

As the name *Happy Science* helps describe very simply, we explore the theme of happiness which humankind has long sought after. And we have added "science" to our name because this happiness shouldn't remain contained within a small scope. We strive to share our ideas and actions with all the different fields of learning and all aspects of human life.

There is, indeed, an extremely broad scope to the happiness we explore, but after all is said and done, the starting point lies within each individual. So I ask you to think very honestly to yourself: When did you feel happiness as your own? Could other people's values have bound you, leading you to ignore the voice within your heart? Although no one can see into your mind, could you have conformed your thoughts unconsciously to others' perspectives and lived with yourself untruthfully? What could have caused you to live in this way? This occurred because measuring and managing your thoughts and actions by an inner yardstick of your own felt too daunting to do. Perhaps it was easier to follow the values and standards other people have set, such as those determined by people who are older or are your superiors at work. But it is very difficult to make self-assessments of your inner world and the thoughts within that arise. In fact, you may even be unable to realize whether your mind is in a state of happiness, which could be a reason you have felt this difficulty.

Please ponder, then: when do you feel happiness and unhappiness? Of course, many different occasions may come to mind, such as a time you were given a promotion, succeeded at something, or received a lot of money. But take a moment to pause and think. These occasions have surely brought you moments of happiness. They have surely brought you opportunities. They were very convincing reasons to persuade yourself of your happiness in life. But have they been essential and sufficient to your happiness? When you consider this question, do you feel there could have been other, more fundamental moments of happiness? Even when you are without wealth, a high position title, or the recognition of the world, you still can have moments of happiness deep within.

Perhaps words cannot describe your feelings in these moments, but they must have welled up from within your depths. What could these feelings have been? They were the clear sense of fulfillment you felt when you had combusted your life energy to its fullest during the hours of a single day. Happiness is when we sense that we've fully combusted our lives in the twenty-four hours of this day, in the same way that oxygen spurs firewood into flames and toward vigorous combustion. This is true not only for you, but also for me. When I look back on my life, I remember that when supreme bliss overcame me, when the greatest happiness filled me, these moments were not always accompanied by results that could be understood by others, and neither could I convincingly explain it to them. In many of these moments, I felt a sense of happiness that words could not express. Authors of classical Japanese literature, such as the writers of *Essays in Idleness* and *The Pillow Book*, captured picturesque moments of nature's seasons in their words to express their feelings. Happiness is like those feelings; it arrives ever so suddenly as an experience purely your own.

To describe my happiness in these moments, I can say first that it came as a supreme moment of calm. It came as a calm stillness that nothing could ever disturb, and there was strength within this inner calm itself that could forbid all disruptions; that's the kind of inner space that was created within me. These are the kind of moments when we experience a sense of oneness with the great universe, even as we live separately as individuals.

Nowadays, people have great difficulty finding such moments. There being all kinds of work chasing after you, one task after another, is one reason that this has happened to you. Rushing is the other reason. As more and more of you live full lives with encounters with many people, moments of inner peace vanish from your lives. Consider today, for example: have even a second or two of inner silence or thoughts of calmness arisen in your mind since you rose from bed this morning? Probably they never crossed your mind. Perhaps today is too short of a period. What would you find if you looked back at the past twelve months? Have any moments during the past year filled your being with inner serenity? What many of you will probably realize is that inner peace has escaped you, even during the end-of-the-year holidays and summer vacation. With so much of your mind directed outward and into busy matters, your mind may have been stuck swinging swiftly back and forth. Even on your days off, you still may not be able to stop this swaying, and then before long, it's time to go back to work again.

Perhaps what's more truthful to say is that you can't help but busy yourself somehow all the time. Could you spend one hour sitting still, doing absolutely nothing? Perhaps you couldn't. You'd probably pick up the newspaper, switch on the television screen, or strike up a conversation with someone. Even an hour of silence probably feels too unbearable to endure. If that's the case, it's a sign that I need to tell you about a profound happiness you have lost sight of.

2

FEELING THE MYSTICAL

Just now, I have talked about the sense of happiness we feel in moments of inner peace. When happiness comes in these moments, where does it come from? It comes from the sense of something otherworldly and sacred. When we are at peace, our minds feel free and unconstrained, so we can easily sense the higher existence.

If human existence resembled ants near the ground, the greatness or the peaceful stillness of the universe would be beyond our ability to describe. The precise length of an ant's lifespan is something I do not know, but as I ponder its existence, I discover that the stars in the sky remain unseen, the sun's existence is never recognized, and the universe remains undiscovered by them, even as they share this time on Earth with us. Discovering this, I realize the great splendor of tasting the kind of happiness that an ant will never be able to. The ground below is everything an ant will ever be capable of seeing in its whole life. Perhaps it will recognize when a rock or a piece of food appears in front of it, but the world of an ant is so tremendously small. The stars in the sky and the moon hanging over a mountain or shining in the lake's reflection will remain beyond an ant's notice. Even the breeze that sweeps atop the lake or the beauty of the setting sun are things of this physical world that an ant can never witness. An ant can never watch birds fluttering on treetops or hear their twittering songs. To an ant, birds are only something huge and fearful, that could swoop down from anywhere at a moment's notice to snatch it up. The beauty of a birdsong might be beyond an ant's understanding.

We, as human beings, are able to appreciate a happiness beyond that of an ant, because we perceive more than just the objects in front of us. Our nature as human beings is not to recognize only what's in front of us. We can cast our thoughts beyond the domain of daily life. When we have inner piece, we are able to discover what is beyond human existence, and the ability to do so leads to a profound happiness. Experiencing this mystical moment is the great happiness endowed to human beings.

At some point in your life, you, too, have savored these moments of happiness. During a hike up a mountain trail, when a panoramic view of spectacular beauty suddenly unfolded before your eyes, what were your feelings? And when you sat down to have a break and you noticed flowers on the trail smiling at you, what did you feel? The clean, fresh air of the mountains must have amazed you. Even the stars probably looked completely different from the stars seen from the rush and bustle of a big city.

At this very moment, those twinkling stars may no longer exist. In the time it took their light to reach your eyes, traveling for hundreds of millions or even tens of billions of light years, those stars may have disappeared. On the planets that circled those stars, human beings like us may have lived, but by the time their light reached your eyes, their civilizations may have long closed their chapters. Some of the light that reached your eyes could have been that of a long-lost civilization. Even if you can sense traces of that civilization right now, it may have already been long ago that it has vanished. When these mystical ruminations arise in me, I am struck by the profound sense that "I am that I am, yet, I am not that I am." I believe this is the sense granted to human beings as the "lords of creation" to savor true happiness.

3

What Happens When You Worry

So far, I have discussed experiences of a mystical kind, and perhaps such experiences feel remote from the everyday reality of your life. But there are many kinds of commonplace experiences. At the end of the day, what kind of day could you look back on and say, "I can end my day in happiness"? Described in a more passive way, it would be a day you could end by saying, "Well, today has gone smoothly again without any sort of grave troubles, incidents, or problems popping up. I didn't get into arguments with anyone, and things worked out very smoothly." Why do you feel so joyful on such days? Because a whole day spent with an unruffled mind is itself a veritable sign of happiness.

If you observe people who are living unhappily, you will find them entrapped by their worries and problems. There will, no doubt, be something that's troubling them in their hearts. These troubles always have a certain characteristic, and that is that they divide your inner world and send your thoughts in two, three, or many directions. In such a distressed state of mind, you become confused and cannot reach a conclusion; this is the nature of a distressed mind. Most of your worries and problems arise from a lack of the information, knowledge, and experience that you are in need of to reach a conclusion under pressure. Most distresses can be explained in this way.

The mind goes through much anguish when we are faced with a worry or a problem; people can go through many years in this state, or at least a couple of weeks to one month. I wish to give you this message to help you through such times in your life: First, you have to notice that you are currently in a state of unhappiness. When you feel your mind wavering frantically, tearing into two, splitting into three, or pulling in every different direction, this, itself, is your unhappiness, so you'll first need to recognize that fact. The reason is that when the mind is in this condition, we're unsuited to otherworldly, mystical experiences, as I have said earlier, and also we are blinded to the beauty within ourselves and others.

Inner distress has a most harmful aspect to it, which is that it makes you blind to beauty, whether this is within yourself, within others, or in this world that you and others share. When you're in the midst of worries the world seems crooked, wrong, and full of contradictions. So you are not happy nor joyful and can't feel a sense of fulfillment in life. Therefore, you must realize that you are currently in this negative state of mind and strive to break free of it as soon as possible, not losing a single day, an hour, or even a minute of time in doing so.

When you see that happiness goes beyond the satisfaction of what's gained and that a great human happiness lies in the calmness of your present mind, you will see there is only one way: maintaining your peace of mind within your given conditions and circumstances of life. This is one way. Our circumstances cannot always be changed exactly as we'd wish. Even if they are going to change eventually, change still takes time to manifest. But even if things won't be able to change immediately, there is still something you can do now, and that is to calm your mind within any circumstance.

When you create this state of mind, you will first attain a moment of happiness, and in that tranquility, you will be able to find yourself celebrating this world and other people again. People who find themselves in the midst of problems are apt to blame other people 99 percent—or, in fact, 100 percent of the time. They will speak ill words and think ill of others. Even if they don't express it verbally, they are finding fault with other people in their thoughts; this is always the case. As a result of this, they suffer through anguish. But you do not want to be in this abject state of blaming your unhappiness on others for too long. You and others are friends, each possessing a unique personality and striving diligently to bloom splendidly in your lives together on this Earth. Perhaps you will meet flowers of colors and shapes that displease you. You may have encounters with flowers of different sizes, or they may not flourish exactly when you would have expected. But like you, they are all making their own efforts to bloom. If there were a single day when you thought ill of them, found fault with them, or found something offensive about them and even cursed their existence, it is something to be ashamed of as a fellow human being. This is a wrong attitude of mind not in just a moral sense, but also because it ruins your own happiness.

4

WAYS TO MAINTAIN PEACE OF MIND

I advise people who are living as egoists to be egoists in the deeper sense. Most egoists, in the common sense of the word, seek self-gain, but they actually do themselves great harm in doing so. We human beings can never be happy by making other people unhappy. This is a very basic principle of life, but one that egoists don't seem to be aware of. In their desire for happiness, they say words that are hurtful, judgmental, and sometimes depraving to others, and they commit acts that bring obstruction and distress to others. But this way of life never leads them to happiness, not just because it's wrongful in the moral sense, but also because we're not able to lead a happy life when we behave in those ways. That's all the more reason why we should refrain from committing such actions.

Therefore, it's crucial for you to learn how to love yourself in the true sense. Numerous people have not learned how to do this. So, what does it mean to love yourself in the true sense? It means living with a sense of fulfillment that you are fully burning your mind's fuel or your given life throughout the day. This is so crucial to your life that you truly should take this to heart.

Therefore, if you wish for happiness, you must first maintain a calm state of mind, like a smooth, polished mirror or the calm surface of a lake. You must maintain the calmness of this mirror and keep it shining. A mirror reflects true images of this world only as long as it preserves a clear surface that is smooth. What would happen if even a single crack were to ever form in it? It would no longer be able to show beautiful images—much less if the mirror is soiled. Only when the mirror is kept clear and shining is it capable of reflecting images of true beauty.

This mirror is within all of us. The daily practice of self-reflection is the equivalent of polishing this mirror. But we must try never to unruffle the lake within our mind. We must keep the surface unshaken, extraordinarily clear, and peaceful, so that the reflection of the moon can be seen upon it. We must sustain this calm lake within us so that it can truthfully reflect the world, others, and, above all, our own selves.

Take Time for Silence

One important way that inner peace is created is through spending time in silence. Each day, find a time of tranquility when not a single word is spoken, and spend that time looking within. This is just one habit to build, but you'll surely feel your sense of happiness arise through it.

These experiences of mine may sound so simplistic that they may make you chuckle. But looking back, I recall that

I have felt strong feelings of happiness during evening walks at dusk, when I'd feel the seasons changing. Some occasions came on a day in autumn, around evenfall. At other times, there would be some red plum blossoms blooming marvelously in the January snow, and I'd be struck by their beauty as I'd catch sight of them. On all these occasions, I'd taste a happiness I had no words to describe, and nothing could ever have replaced this bliss.

This experience can be described as a heightened sense of fulfillment or a peak experience; it is a feeling that's very close to the state of enlightenment in Zen Buddhism. It is by a curious fact that those who have had such blissful experiences, people who have gone through this heightened sense of happiness, have decided to live for the sake of others from that point forward. This is true historically. In the past, many have experienced this feeling growing strongly within them after these moments of supreme bliss. In my understanding, they must have felt a oneness with the universe and discovered that they are loved by a great existence. This feeling of bliss filling their whole being must have awakened their desire to help as many people as possible have the same kind of experience. This feeling cannot but grow within you when you've tasted such a true happiness. What I am advising you to do is not anything special: please create the mirror-like surface of a lake within you. Maintaining this state of mind will, in itself, bring you joy.

Do Not Get Angry

No one has the right to make others unhappy. Or, to put it another way, you do not need to be made miserable by what others do. You can choose your own happiness or unhappiness. So, have a mindset that's resolved to protect the mirror-like surface of your mind, because this mindset itself will create changes in your mental attitude toward people around you in the most natural way.

When you allow yourself to get upset by trivial things, you prevent yourself from maintaining calmness within your mind. We are often taught that we shouldn't get angry, and there is a reason for this teaching besides the moral aspect. Anger ripples the surface of your inner lake and creates a feeling of unpleasantness that disturbs your very happiness.

Anger arises when you feel treated unfairly; you respond to this feeling with anger out of your desire to be happy, but you destroy something most dear to you in doing so. Whenever such a desire to protect yourself arises from within you, hold your ground for a moment and look at the lake within. Realize that you are on the verge of destroying something most valuable to you in this moment. The moment you fly into a rage to protect yourself, you are standing on the edge of a precipice, risking a fall into an abyss from the mountain you have spent so long climbing. If you aspire to develop yourself as a person and seek happiness, you should never give in to brutish anger.

You may not feel convinced by what I say, and you may feel like saying, "The world is full of injustices, and many wrongs seem to go on prevailing. In some cases, misunderstandings also occur. Won't a lot of harm be caused if these misunderstandings are not resolved?" You may have valid reasons for being upset, because there are two types of anger: anger for personal interest and anger against social injustice. I am saying you must avoid the first type, the anger that protects yourself. The other type, the anger based on a rational and righteous perspective, is a necessary part of constructing an ideal world and preventing evil from gaining power. When you feel you must take action to correct a situation, you must act rationally, in the understanding that it is a form of love of making others notice their mistakes. If you fully understand the difference between flying into a rage and reproaching others, you will not lose your inner peace.

In this world, there are two kinds of responsibility: direct responsibility and indirect responsibility. If someone criticizes you for causing something to happen, you cannot run away. You must face up squarely to your direct responsibility.

On the other hand, there are many cases in which you must assume indirect responsibility for a situation that came about as a result of your carelessness, your lack of effort, or, in a broader sense, your lack of strength of character or virtue. If you have not been caring for others on a daily basis or spending your time fostering their happiness, sometimes you will need to pay the debt. If you are suffering because you have been mis-understood, think in terms of direct and indirect responsibility, and consider whether some aspect of indirect responsibility deserves more self-reflection.

If you see that someone has thrown a stone into your inner lake, try to stop the ripples from spreading. Make the effect as small as possible. Stay calm, for sometimes you may need to answer words of hatred with silence.

Cultivate a Tolerant Heart

At times, you may meet people who act in a way that you couldn't have imagined a human being acting, and you may find yourself unable to forgive them. At times like this, try to think in this way: "That person has parents and maybe much-loved children. He must have friends who see him as good and worthy of their admiration. I may be committing a big mistake by writing off his whole character. I am not always necessarily right, and he is not always necessarily wrong or bad." It is very important to bear in mind this perspective and doing so is a heart of tolerance.

Practicing the virtue of tolerance is important not just in the moral sense and because it puts others at ease; it is also of great value in keeping the lake within you undisturbed, and this ensures lasting happiness. Just as you are not perfect, neither are others. Have you ever heard the saying, "If you are friends with everyone's good side, you will never meet a bad person"? When you are enraged by someone, can you remember this person's good and exceptional points?

Once you have learned about inner serenity, you need to be extremely careful not to fly into a rage or write off someone's entire character. Misunderstandings will eventually be resolved. There is a Buddhist saying: "Resentment cannot be healed through resentment." I believe that even if you feel that you have suffered at the hands of others, you must not nurse resentment in your heart. It is love that will work things out. What heals grudges is compassion like the sun that constantly provides warmth and light.

Give Things Time

In discussing inner serenity, I would like to bring your attention to something that is extremely important: patience that withstands the test of time. Most of your sufferings and mistakes are born of wanting to jump to conclusions in a short period of time, while actually, a long amount of time is given to us in this life. Although a person may seem to be an enemy now, in a year's time he or she may be your friend. Since people can change, you have to believe in that possibility, and that requires you to persevere in the present.

If you have a tendency to label people "good" or "bad," this is something to be cautious about doing. If you see certain qualities in a person and quickly conclude that the person is "bad" and give him or her this label, it may give you a sense of relief. But in doing this, you forestall the possibility of making friends with this person. This is the same as throwing away a precious treasure. You can only meet a limited number of people in one lifetime, no matter how many contacts you may have. Even a politician, who goes on campaign tours around the country, probably does not meet very many people he can have a heart-to-heart talk with.

If there's emotional friction between you and someone else and your personalities clash, it means that you have some kind of significant spiritual connection with this person. Often, this person is appearing in your life because you need him or her for the training of your soul. By taking the view that there are no coincidences in this world, you can come to recognize that there is value in the relationship. It is important to think that this person's words could be teaching you something, perhaps about something lacking in yourself. Human beings aren't always saintly and perfect, and when someone is causing you distress, it may be difficult to forgive the person right at that instant. I have a word of advice for times like this: give this person time. Deciding to at least give the person time is something you can do in such difficult moments.

Everything that exists in this universe is on its way of evolving. We are all living in the same times together, but each individual is progressing at a different speed of soul growth. It's not necessary for this person to have the same knowledge as you. People may be where you were ten years ago or where you will be three years from now. Each person lives in his or her own flow of time. If you can think, "Given enough time, something might happen to change this person for the better; perhaps a change will be inspired by this encounter with me," then it wouldn't be fair not to give this possibility a chance.

Apologize Sincerely

When you hurt someone with words, you will immediately see the reaction on the other person's face and in their eyes. If you think you have caused ripples, giving your sincere apology is very important. What you said may be right, or it may have actually been beneficial for this person, but it is still important to apologize for your harsh remarks, since they have upset the person. Apologize for hurting the person, and to make amends, say something more. Lose no time in explaining what you truly meant, to calm the other person's heart and mind.

When you encounter people whose minds are full of depressed thoughts, people who are very distressed, or people who are spilling over with complaints, you can do something to help them regain the happiness of inner peace. First of all, you should look for the reason their mind is in distress, for there is always a cause. They must be worried about something. It's important to nip the worry in the bud. Even if you do not have the ability to do this, words and thoughts still have definite power.

When you see people who are always distressed about their poor health, you may worry about meeting them, because it could cause ripples to form in your mind. But rather than thinking only of protecting your own peace of mind, if you can see that they're worrying about their health, you could also do something to cheer them up. You could offer words that would give them happiness. You could look for ways to offer inner calm to the people you meet throughout the day, whatever the reason is that brings you together. Without doubt, you truly *can*. Through your thoughts and words, people can be changed in a moment. This is simply the truth.

The human mind can be shaken by the slightest disturbance. So we should also recognize that not only are stones thrown into our inner lakes, but also we throw stones into the lakes of others, and we should determine never to disturb the happiness of others. This is our sacred obligation as people. It sounds so simple, but maintaining peace of mind is extremely important for people living in our times. There are millions and tens of millions of people who cannot do this.

Ask a person in distress whether his or her mind is at peace. The response you'll receive will be "No." If you ask why not, the person will give you a number of reasons. Then, if you continue to ask, "I understand your reasons. I wonder, though, is it truly not possible to create inner peace unless these conditions change?" By asking this person in this way, he or she will start to see that it is possible. The causes of distress may or may not be solved over time, but at least the person can calm his or her presently troubled mind.

5

LIKE A WARM AUTUMN DAY

In this chapter, I have discussed a simple subject, but this discussion could easily be expanded into a more difficult and philosophical discussion by referring to the Buddhist teachings of the Eightfold Path or the Six Paramita. Here, I have explained the theme in the simplest way.

The basic practice of self-reflection is to constantly check whether your mind is unruffled; you can judge this for yourself. Maintain a calm state, and if you find your mind disturbed during the day, make an effort to calm it. If you have succeeded in maintaining inner calm and your mind is like a warm autumn day throughout the day and for many days at a time, that means that you have spent that time in happiness. Wishing to help others attain the same state will lead to further self-development and happiness for you.

I have spoken as simply as possible in this chapter. Please take to heart this one word of advice I've been giving: *create peace in your mind*. In time, you will gradually realize that it is not so easy to do, and you will find that simply by practicing peace in your mind, you will develop greatness as a person before you know it.

I am convinced that through your own practice, you will eventually understand that this single point summarizes my teachings, including all the things I've talked about over the course of more than a hundred books.*

---

* Since the day this lecture was given in 1989, Ryuho Okawa has continued to provide many more lectures and books, numbering more than 3,000 lectures and over 2,600 titles as of November 2019.

CHAPTER THREE

REBUILDING YOUR LIFE

1

Resentment Cannot Be Healed through Resentment

I have chosen to entitle this chapter, "Rebuilding Your Life." You may be wondering what I may intend to discuss under this theme. Were I to begin this chapter with the concluding message I wish to give to you, it would be that there are indeed misfortunes, failures, and setbacks in life, but your journey to happiness can begin from within any kind of circumstance. We want to think on these words, and this is the main message I wish to give in this chapter.

The first thing I wish to tell you is this teaching in Buddhism: resentment cannot be healed through resentment. This is just a single sentence—yet how numerous are the people who fail to understand it. When faced with suffering, sadness, illness, or adversity, we cannot help but want to blame things other than ourselves. When we do, we are running away from the person we should ideally be, and some of us allow these feelings to develop into active resentment against others.

For example, in Japan, the unjustified dropping of the atomic bombs brought death to a hundred thousand people or perhaps even more, and there are people to this day who are still suffering from serious illnesses because of their effects. I imagine that the hearts of the families and descendants of these victims cannot have had any inner peace. Honestly speaking, some among them must have feelings of resentfulness that I have just described. When an unexplainable event beyond your control completely changes your life and the lives of others, especially in the direction of difficult circumstances, we cannot help but feel strong unforgivingness and resentment toward the person or nation that's responsible for the event. It's only natural that we react this way.

But happiness escapes those who are resentful, and so does success. This is the first point I would like to make. Do you know why this is the case? Directing your inner pain out to the world may seem to bring a sense of relief. But carrying a resentful heart within you throughout your life is akin to unknowingly drinking poison, such as arsenic, day after day. Whatever kind of reason underlies your resentment, and even if you feel your feelings are justified from the point of view of justice, this is still not the way we human beings were made to live, and it is not your path to happiness. The reason is that at the very essence of a resentful heart there lies a desire for misfortune to befall others. Whatever may be your basis for these feelings, the mind that wishes to harm others opposes the heart of God. Such thoughts not only reach them, but also come back to affect you.

This is a spiritual principle that exists. In the world of our mind, there is actually a set of principles from which no one can ever escape. This set of principles stands firmly as a singular pillar of guiding values for this universe. Those whose thoughts and deeds stay within this golden pillar are promised eternal growth and progress. But the thoughts and deeds that leave this golden pillar, those that stray from this golden tunnel, do not contribute to the growth of your soul—just as if we jump out of a spaceship with our lifeline cut off, we will simply float in outer space, unable to move ahead or in any intended direction. Such is a fact.

Approximately forty-five years ago,* two Japanese men in midget submarines were traveling the ocean floor, making their way toward Sydney Harbor, Australia. Loaded upon the nose of each of these special submarines was a bomb. And within the submarines, the men would forever be enclosed, because the hatches were shut permanently. These were the submarines on kamikaze missions. One of them, regrettably, came to a halt underwater due to a mishap; never would this submarine fulfill its mission. But the other submarine continued its course and eventually drove into an Australian cargo ship in the bay. The impact not only killed the man in the submarine, but also caused the cargo ship to explode and sink.

---

* The approximate number of years traced back from 1993, the year the Japanese edition of this book was published.

How did the Australian people react to this event? They were astonished, not only by the sinking of the cargo ship, but also by the bravery of the Japanese marines who had sacrificed their lives in this attack. Later, the Australians set up a memorial for these unnamed, courageous Japanese marines.

So it was not resentment that filled the hearts of the Australian people whose cargo ship had been sunk. Their hearts were instead filled with deep respect for the fallen men and their spirit of self-sacrifice. In this reaction, I saw that these Australian people possessed something beyond just a sense of good and evil or a sense of justice; I saw something beyond thinking of only personal self-interest or distinctions between friend and foe. Although recent times have seen strong diplomatic ties between Japan and Australia, until the 1960s the Australian sentiment toward the Japanese was less than amicable. It was in spite of the sentiments of the times that the Australian people chose to build this monument.

The Australians' hearts were moved by neither the country of Japan nor the Japanese people as a whole; instead it was the two men who had perished. I saw, in this event, a difference in mental attitude, a heart that surpassed thoughts of personal interest to pay tribute to the human character.

There are countless episodes that speak to this theme, but explaining each one persuasively in a way that others will understand can be a difficult task. For example, the recent visit of the Korean president caused a domestic dispute here in

Japan, because he requested a formal apology for Japan having invaded his country in the past. This subject can be viewed in many ways. Seen from the Japanese standpoint, giving an apology could be an admirable deed of its own right. But there is something about this that does not feel right to me. It relates to what I said earlier: resentment is not healed through resentment. However much you dwell on the unchangeable past and wish to change it, it is difficult to do. Instead, what is most important is how you assess the event and how you will put the lessons gained to good use. It is the lessons that we learn and putting them to use that are vital. Feelings of hate and resentment within our mind exist beyond time, itself, in fact, and persist in the present. They do not become things of the past, but endure in the present. This is why, when we hold onto these feelings, we are always unable to advance on the path to happiness. This is an astonishing truth so many people do not realize.

I will tell you about another example. Blessed with abundant fields of cotton, India used to have a very prosperous spinning industry. After the British colonized India, however, they needed to purchase raw cotton and tea leaves from India, which meant that they have to pay in foreign currency and, therefore, needed Indians to purchase British goods. This resulted in the destruction of India's spinning industry by the British. The British forced the Indians to buy British-made cotton products and limited India to selling only raw cotton.

The British even went as far as cutting off the arms of cotton spinners in India.

This is actually one of the reasons why India has not succeeded at modernization. This event caused India to fail to industrialize and is clearly one of the reasons the country has remained stagnant. I do not know how the people of India now feel about this history of their country. But forty to fifty years after India won back its independence, if they continue to hold grudges about this past event, their country's chance of modernizing in the future will be slight. For India to become a modern nation, there is no other way but for the people of India themselves to leave behind their past, take up the spirit of entrepreneurship, and make earnest efforts to pave their path.

A similar situation occurred in China. After World War II, the Chinese also missed their opportunity to modernize their country. During Mao Zedong's administration, authorities attributed their country's poor quality of life to Japan's invasion of China, insisting that it had brought devastation to their country. The Chinese people were thus encouraged by their leaders to resent Japan for their poverty. At first, the people of China believed this story, but in the late '70s, they started to doubt. Seeing the prosperous growth achieved by the Taiwanese people, some of whom are ethnically Chinese, the people of China could no longer let that be their excuse. The people who live and work in Taiwan have the same Chinese ethnicity as those of the mainland. But Taiwan's per capita GNP was at least sixteen times greater than China's (as of 1992-1993). The people of China could no longer avoid wondering how Taiwan's GNP could be so different from theirs.

Hong Kong, which is now governed by Britain, is also very prosperous.* Since the colony is scheduled to revert to the governance of mainland China before the end of the twentieth century, the Chinese residents of Hong Kong are now escaping overseas. They are obtaining Canadian citizenship or citizenship from other countries and setting up their business addresses in Hong Kong. They are also of the same Chinese origin, but they are afraid of being absorbed back into mainland China after 1997. What is the issue here?

The issue is the government itself. These events are a matter of political success and failure, and this is the reason that China started on the path toward modernization belatedly, in the latter half of the '70s, by incorporating economic reforms.

---

* The dates and factual information in the original 1993 Japanese edition have been kept.

2

The First Step:
Stopping the Negative
Thoughts in Your Mind

I have described some events of the twentieth century that have impacted various countries. I'd like to say that similar experiences constantly occur in the lives of individuals. For example, suppose that in your life so far, you have not seen any success and have not had much happiness. If I were to ask you why, you would surely have some kind of explanation. You would have a reason to help you explain your lack of success—I am certain about that. Perhaps if you are in your early adulthood, your reason would be your poor performance on your college entrance exams—perhaps your life has veered off since that happened. If you are slightly older, you may point to a setback in marriage—maybe a loved one refused your marriage proposal, or maybe your marriage had no sooner begun when it started to fall apart. Or perhaps your new business went under after just a year or two. These are possible examples.

If you asked this question of each person, everyone would definitely have an answer of one kind or another, and probably 80 to 90 percent would point to external causes. This is nearly always the case with anyone who has not yet come to know the

Truths. There are some exceptions, of course; a few fortunate people who have been raised well or have been surrounded by thoughtful friends may have learned how to reflect upon themselves. But most people with a failed business will explain to you that they placed their trust in the wrong person, they faced trouble caused by an employee, the interest rate on their loans suddenly rose, or something happened with their client. Always looking to find the cause outside themselves, they will give you various reasons like these.

Suppose that the man you imagined marrying says that he is breaking up with you to date another woman. How would you react? Would you lay the blame on your ex-boyfriend for being unfaithful to you? Or would you accuse the woman who stole his heart away from you? Somewhere within your heart, you would probably have these feelings, whatever your reaction would turn out to be. Somewhere within your heart would lie a desire to find fault with his unfaithfulness or to accuse the woman who seduced his heart.

But in letting out these dismal, destructive feelings of resentment, you would be allowing happiness to escape from you. You would be letting yourself go down the path of further misery.

Suppose you have made a new acquaintance, and she has told you her story of the misery of her life. Ever since she and her husband faced bankruptcy ten years ago, they have suffered through life's bitter hardships as they've watched their debts accumulate endlessly. When you hear her story for the first time, your heart feels deep sympathy. But when she tells you the same story the next time you see her, you may dread hearing her woes again. How will you feel, then, if she tells you the same story the third time you see her? Your feelings of sympathy may turn into doubt, and you may wonder to yourself, "Why has she stayed so miserable? Why hasn't she started on a new path yet?"

By holding on to past misfortunes, she is not seeking happiness, in the end. In holding on tightly to her misery and cherishing it, she infects others with her atmosphere of gloom; by prompting other people's moods to grow somber and their hearts to grow depressed, she makes them unconsciously avoid her. Because of the saddened feelings that grow when they spend time with her, they begin seeing her much less often.

So she laments, "I've suffered so much, but no one has shown me much sympathy. Worse still, people keep farther and farther away from me, and no one seems to want to listen. How full this world is of cold-hearted people. Is there not a shred of compassion in anyone's heart?" Through thoughts such as these, her unhappiness reproduces over and over. People make themselves into tragic heroes in this typical way, generating misfortune for themselves and not realizing the principles of the mind.

I have emphasized repeatedly that hatred, jealousy, dissatisfaction, and complaint may seem to arise naturally in your mind, but by unleashing them, you're allowing the beasts that have been born in your mind to escape from your mouth. These wild beasts that you let loose—hatred, jealousy, dissatisfaction, and complaint—will not only harm others; they will also return to bite you. We need to be aware of this fact and stop it. Because the relationships we build with one another are a basis of this world, the words of harm that we express eventually come back to us. So, if you are experiencing a terrible life crisis or adversity and you are filled with thoughts of complaint, you must first cease having these negative thoughts. If you are generating unhappy thoughts and unleashing these beasts onto the streets, you must build a fence to keep them in—otherwise, they will bring harm to you and others.

You must fence them in and cease housing them in your mind. You must stop them resolutely. No matter how much unhappiness has filled your past, the sympathy you seek will not bring you happiness. If seeking sympathy gives you feelings of happiness, this happiness will only be superficial, paper-thin, and fragile and will turn into an addiction that will become difficult to resist. It will lead you to spend your life chasing people's sympathy and will gradually destroy you. Dwelling on self-pity is a path that leads nowhere; this is something you must realize.

It does not matter how much you convince yourself of your unhappiness. Doing so does not lead anywhere; it will only lead to a dead end. This is so important to realize. Please try to realize this fact. For when you realize this, you will start to see that those negative thoughts you have had were actually the desire to receive, or to take from others, transposed. In the end, you were looking to receive from others. With a voracious appetite in your heart, you have been constantly asking for this thing or that thing, like an antlion pit—a sandy trap that swallows all kinds of things but is never filled up; a pit like a cone-shaped mortar that endlessly draws everything into itself, like a black hole.

What will become of this world if it becomes full of people whose minds are like an antlion's pit? Just imagine seeing the streets lined with such pits, ones with human faces that appear when they open their mouths wide and you look at them closely. It will be difficult to walk down the streets peacefully, seeing the hands reaching out of the ground and trying to drag you in, trying to take from you. What will the world be like if it becomes filled with people like this? I have just given you an image, but in the other world, where you will return as a spirit after death, this kind of place really exists.

There is a place in the other world where hands are reaching out of the ground, trying to drag people in. There really are people who try to gain happiness by doing such things. This place is found in the world called Hell, and is definitely not a place of happiness. Not only do these people live without happiness, but they also create unhappiness for the people around them. Just think, if everyone around you is becoming unhappy, who will give you happiness? Only the happy are capable of giving you happiness.

Those who are happy are the very people who can bring you happiness, who are able to save you. People suffering from unhappiness cannot possibly save you. If you seek to be saved and to become happy, it's vital for you to increase the number of happy people. However full of pain, needfulness, and dissatisfaction your present circumstances may seem to you, cease seeing your circumstances in these ways, and approach them in this way instead: "I am under difficult circumstances right now; it's true. But I wonder what I can do, even while I find myself in the midst of them? What can I achieve from within these less-than-adequate circumstances that presently surround me? There must be something I can do. At the very least, there must be a way I can make myself useful to the world or a way I can bring happiness to other people. However difficult my circumstances may seem, I resolve never to become like the ant in the pit. If I ever become like one, and if I ever find myself surrounded by many other pits in this world, then I will shout until my last breath. I will warn passersby to watch their step and avoid my pit. Even if this is the only job remaining to me, this is what I will do."

At least, when you wish to increase the number of people who share your suffering, you're living with a heart of cowardice. As you face your suffering, you need to think to yourself, "I need to stop the spread of this suffering. No other person should ever have to undergo this kind of suffering or experience these feelings." This is the way to prevent others from suffering in these pits, and they, in turn, will then be able to save other people who suffer from unhappiness. That is right. However miserable you find your circumstances to be, you must strive to create happy people.

You must abandon negative thoughts, generate positive thoughts in their place, and search constantly for ways to help others find happiness. Even when you're ill, you can still bring happiness to others. In the same way that an ill physician can still heal patients, even you, who are facing severe hardship at this moment, can use your words to guide others who have not yet seen the kind of hardship you face. If you are unable to practice acts of kindness toward others, you are thinking of yourself much too often. You have been too immersed in matters concerned with yourself. It's something you will need to stand back from a little bit.

Bring your attention to your surroundings. Observe the many other people that surround you. There are a great number of people out there doing their best to live their lives. Why have you turned a blind eye to this fact? There are other people living their lives in earnest, and you must turn your gaze to their efforts. This is something important that you must do. There are multitudes of other people in different circumstances who are making an effort in life. You must not forget to think of them.

3

THE SECOND STEP: THE STUDY OF PEOPLE

I have explained that the first step to rebuilding your life is to cast out negative mindsets—such as the heart of resentment, the heart of cursing your circumstances, and the heart of blaming others—then, the second step is to practice the study of people.

Do not merely observe within yourself; also observe your surroundings. Deeply observe the world around you. Observe the people who live in this world and what they are like, the problems they bear, and the feelings they live with. These are the things that you must come to know more and more of now.

Take a moment now to consider the people around you. If you have seen your marriage crumble, lost a parent, been stricken with illness, or failed an exam, you have not been alone in that experience. Many other people from many walks of life have shared these experiences, and yet, the paths these different people have taken through them have varied and we want to earnestly study the reasons behind their differences. When we do, we want to pay special attention to two kinds of people: the unhappy and the successful.

Studying the Unhappy

First, we want to study the cause of people's unhappiness. At your job, in your home, or somewhere else within immediate sight or hearing distance, there must be someone suffering from unhappiness. If there is an unhappy person nearby whom you can study with some ease, you will not find it too hard to recognize what is causing their unhappiness. This is the easier of the two types to study. Practice a study of this person. What could be the cause of this person's unhappiness? What could be the reason for their repeated mistakes? What could be at the root of their unhappiness?

As you ponder these questions, you will discover a number of reasons. Which among them stands out as the main one? For example, perhaps you know someone who has repeatedly faced failure in his business. These failures may have been caused by a variety of reasons, such as a bad economy, his trusting the wrong person, insufficient financing, or the poor quality of his employees. But on close examination, you may find the true reason to have been his own tendency to be impatient. He is always irritable and in a hurry. And in his state of hastiness, his trust in other people's work falters, his irritability rises, and he begins to interfere in their work. In this state, he feels rushed to produce quick results. With some additional patience he could actually reach success, but when things don't turn out as well as he had hoped as quickly as he would like, he suddenly throws in the towel, in spite of the money that's gone into his business and all the people who work for him. And by throwing in the towel so suddenly, he completely loses the trust-based relationships he has built over the course of years, all in a single day. This is something that some people do. Ultimately, a heart of impatience lacks sufficient breathing room to truly consider others. There is little room to notice others' circumstances or recognize their situations. A heart of impatience is when our hands are always full of concerns about ourselves and we are constantly filled with anxiety. And out of hastiness, we strive to somehow produce results quickly.

There are also those who fumble just as they reach the verge of success. They may have made considerable progress and successfully come 80 to 90 percent of the way, but then they blunder when they're just inches from success. This type of mistake is often an inadvertent slip of the lip. Out of a sense of relief in the final stage of negotiating a contract, you blurt out a problem that's been troubling your business. You let slip that your warehouse is packed with unsold merchandise or that a loan application was recently turned down and that doing business with them will be a big help. But the other party becomes concerned when they hear this, feels ill at ease, and decides to reassess their decision. After further research, they find that business with you would involve considerable risk, so they decide to decline your contract. Many people in the world make this type of mistake.

Inadvertently, people say things when they're on the brink of success, as if to purposely bring failure upon themselves. Deep inside the hearts of people of this type is actually the unconscious wish to fail. It may upset them to hear me say this—that they are actually seeking failure—but this is really how they appear from an outside person's perspective. During critical situations, people of this type do things that invite failure, and when failure results, they feel relief in confirming to themselves about their unhappiness.

These people are immersed in a bath of lukewarm water, which could give them a cold. But being fearful of the cold that they could catch out in the open air, they always return to the tub's waters. With feelings like this within them, they repeatedly invite failure, and in tasting the same hardships over and over, they confirm their sense of the difficulties of life. When you study other people's failures, their example can teach you many things, so study these types of people well. They will give you many useful lessons to use when placed in a similar position or circumstances in the future. This is why studying others well is so valuable.

Studying the Successful

Another aspect of the study of people is also essential but may be slightly more difficult than examining and studying those who live in unhappiness. This is the study of those who are successful.

It's so important to study successful people. This task can be difficult, that is for certain. Often, the successful have exceeded us in some respects. Because of their exceptional skills, abilities, knowledge, experience, and other qualities, it can be difficult to fully understand their way of thinking. But there is an important attitude that can help us study the successful, and that is to never feel jealous of them.

We should refrain from uttering criticism or ill remarks about them out of envious feelings. This is a very important advice to follow. From having given counsel to and observed many people, I have come to clearly recognize why some people have been unsuccessful. There are exceptional people who are aware that they are exceptional and have been recognized by others as exceptional but have yet to become successful. On examining them, you'll find that the cause always boils down to a single point: they have a mind within that demeans successful people's achievements, because they feel defeated when others become more exceptional and capable than themselves. People who have this mind within them are unfortunately incapable of succeeding, even if they are exceptional people. They walk themselves into failure eventually.

It's difficult for these people to recognize this about themselves. They have great difficulty noticing this. When they see someone succeed, they see them as having wheedled their way to success; this is how they think. And because they take this view of other's successes, they are unable to recognize that the problem behind their lack of success lies within themselves. When you take the view of another's success as the lucky result of wheedling, you deny that it can be material for your further growth. Can you see what I am saying? We often hear people say, "He must have had a lucky break" or "She must be very good at swimming with the tide." But if your aim is to achieve happiness and success, you do not want to utter these words.

You need to discard the mindset that attributes others' successes to causes other than their own efforts and believes nothing is there to be learned of. Feelings of this kind—the cowardice of devaluing another person's efforts—will hinder you from learning from successful people's good points.

Although they're successful, those who've succeeded are not perfect people. Your character may be superior to theirs in some respects. But if someone you know has been successful, acknowledge their success and find the valuable lessons within it; this is part of the path to your own success. Nitpicking and criticizing another person's success may be a temporary consolation, but it makes your own success unachievable and your own happiness unattainable. It is most dangerous to hold onto jealous emotions; jealousy is an emotion that needs to be eliminated from your mind. This emotion of jealousy is the very reason that success has escaped a great many people.

There are people who feel deep sympathy toward the defeated and weak such as the famous Japanese warrior Minamoto No Yoshitsune. There are times when these feelings contain righteousness, when we look at things from the perspective of justice. But from the perspective of the principle of happiness, a constant fondness for the unsuccessful will eventually lead to a love of unhappiness and become a definite impediment to your success. It's important to feel tenderness and compassion toward the unsuccessful and defeated, but you should not let these feelings take root as a tendency in your mind, for if you do, they will make it difficult for you to achieve true self-improvement.

In the end, it's very important to keep learning from those who have been successful and are strong and exceptional. Japan's postwar success can probably be attributed to several causes, but the first was the self-reflection the Japanese people practiced as a result of their defeat. After accepting their mistakes, instead of nursing resentment against the Americans, the Japanese people sought to help Japan grow into a country like the United States. They looked to the United States as their example. In their hearts, they kept saying to themselves, "We want to become like them. We want our people to become like their people," and they worked hard toward this goal. They did not hold on to the resentment of defeat. In fact, they did the opposite: they looked to the United States as a model country and sought to emulate it.

It's my belief that this was the greatest driving force that led Japan to its success. If the Japanese people had continued to blame Japan's devastation on the atomic bombings by the United States, Japan would not have prospered in the way that it did. Instead, they used the practice of self-reflection as leverage and strove to strengthen their country into one like the United States. This, I think, was one of the secrets of Japan's success.

The same circumstance holds true for us as individuals. When you see people who have become successful and happy, you must not do anything to diminish or devalue their happiness. Instead, celebrate their success and happiness; approach them with a heart that wishes to congratulate them. It is this attitude that allows you to learn humbly from others. When someone else achieves success at a time when you are faced with failure, the first thing you must do is, at the least, not speak ill of them. But that alone is not enough; you must also give them words of commendation. Please commend and congratulate them and thank them for being an exceptional example for you. This is exactly the way to turn these situations into learning and growing experiences for yourself. And if you wish to be like this person, then affirm the image they give you of what an ideal person might be like. By affirming them as a role model, you will walk the path to becoming like them.

Let's suppose that you have made some kind of mistake. Maybe it was a business failure. When your child reaches adulthood and begins building a business of his or her own, you should draw on this same advice. When a parent says to his child, "All businesses are made to fail, so yours is bound to fail too," this makes it likely for the child to repeat the parent's failure. But a child becomes successful under a parent who says, "I myself have failed, but many others out in the world have succeeded. There are businesses in the world that have succeeded. Learn well from them, and make your business successful, too." This is how things often work. That is to say, the parent's desire for their child's success or failure affects the child's results. When the parent desires the child's failure, the child walks into the path of failure, bringing further misery upon the parent. We need to be careful of this kind of feeling, which is often found at a subconscious level.

4

THE THIRD STEP: THE CULTIVATION OF IDEALS AND PASSION

In discussing how to rebuild your life, I have talked first about stopping the negative thoughts in your mind. Second, I have spoken about studying others' successes and failures for the various causes behind them. As a natural consequence of this study, you will use your findings to reflect on yourself: "How do these things apply to me? From an objective standpoint, how do I appear? Will my current state of mind, way of life, and abilities actually lead me to happiness and to success? When I think about it, perhaps such and such about myself is something to be careful about. In terms of my personality, maybe such and such aspect of me is something I should watch out for. And maybe I should be cautious about such and such in my approach to my work. And in human relationships, maybe it's such and such aspect of myself that I need to watch out for. Judging from the successful people I've observed, I believe that changing such and such aspect of myself in such and such a way is the right course for me to take." Learn these things, and engrave them into your mind firmly. It is extremely important to have a mind that practices the study of others. A further step is necessary, however.

When you have stopped holding onto negative thoughts and have deeply studied the successes and failures in others, the next thing to do, of course, is set out on your path of self-growth. You must choose this path of further self-development. What must you do when you arrive at this step? What is the most important thing you must have at this time? The answer to these questions is to develop aspirations and ideals. Aspirations and ideals are now the most important things for you to cultivate within yourself. Without aspirations, your growth and progress will stall, in spite of all the effort you have put into studying others.

So the study of others' successes and unhappiness must be followed by the development of your aspirations. Resolve to move forward on your own path with your ideals set high. This ability to envision ideals and set high aspirations is among the greatest of talents bestowed on human beings. Even if you have not yet seen successful outcomes, and have not had them in the past, your ability to hold onto your high aspirations regardless of it is an exceptional talent. Maintaining aspirations is a talent in itself. Realize that you still have this innate talent within you; your ability to aspire is where everything begins. Unhappiness may come to chisel away at your spirit, but you must stop the negative thoughts that arise within you, whatever shape they may take, and instead learn from others carefully, come to know yourself deeply, and burn with an enthusiasm for your ideals.

To further your development, raise your aspirations. This is very important. Those who don't think in this way end up finding it very difficult to move ahead even one step. Some people are very intelligent and good-natured but are not able to succeed. Good-natured people practice the first step, avoiding holding on to resentment. A good-natured person doesn't blame or criticize others. Intelligent people practice the second step, earnestly studying others. But somehow, many earnest and intelligent people are not succeeding. What these people lack is often an aspiration.

It is your ideals that calls forth the passion from within you. And it's people with aspirations that attract other people. Some people ask, "What can I do to develop aspirations?" Others ask, "What can I do to develop a burning enthusiasm for ideals?" Still others ask, "What can I do to live my life with passion?" If just a single person with passion emerges from among these people to become an example, that will be enough to answer all these questions. If, from among the people who read this book, just one person with high aspirations emerges to show how one person can live a life with passion, it will make all further explanation unnecessary.

It's really true. Aspirations hold the power to influence. They hold the power to influence other people. A person with an aspiration exudes an energy and a willfulness that can move the hearts of other people, and amazingly, that aspiration comes to dwell inside them, too. When other people catch onto that energy, they start to want to live that way themselves.

If you've come to know this truth, why not think of becoming an example yourself, rather than seeking to find an example in others? When you're in the pit of despair, at the lowest point of defeat, keep on living brightly in spite of your circumstances. Don't allow negative thoughts into your mind, study others, devise new ways, and challenge yourself once more. Then live out your life with a high aspiration.

Showing others how you have chosen to live in this way is the true secret to helping other people succeed. The condition of greatness is a burning desire that never stops flowing. Any number of circumstances and events may lead you into feelings of self-degradation. There are endless reasons to feel bad about some aspect of yourself, whether it be a physical attribute or an innate ability. This world is overflowing with imperfections that we can use to feel bad. But this is not what matters. Despite these imperfections, and even if our life circumstances seem to surround us with rubbish, we must dare to live like the beautiful crane. This is the test we are given and a very important task. The more people there are who can live this way, the more this world will be filled with people who can do great things. People who are good-natured or intelligent but unhappy need to find a burning enthusiasm. When you encounter this type of person in your life, please tell them about the importance of having passion, for this is the key that will open the door to their happiness.

5

The Fourfold Path and Rebuilding Your Life

At Happy Science, I teach the Principles of Happiness, which consist of the Fourfold Path of Love, Wisdom, Self-Reflection, and Progress. The first step to rebuilding your life—discarding negative thinking—corresponds to the teaching of love, which promotes the practice of giving love to others. In this practice, we put an end to taking love from others and having attachments, and we practice giving love instead.

The second step, the study of other people, corresponds to the teachings of wisdom and self-reflection. This step is ultimately about deep wisdom, which can also be described as knowledge of the Truths. This step also contains aspects of self-reflection, especially intellectual self-reflection. Finally, developing aspirations corresponds to the teaching of progress.

If you eliminate dark thoughts, live with bright thoughts in their place, earnestly study other people, and maintain aspirations throughout your life, you will never know failure, but only happiness. I hope that with these three steps, each one of you will be able to rebuild your life. I have only the greatest of expectations for everyone.

CHAPTER FOUR

LIVING
IN
ETERNITY
NOW

1

PERCEPTIONS OF TIME

In this chapter entitled "Living in Eternity Now," I would like to talk about a theory of time. What has been your perception of time? Time is a notion that most people closely associate with the clock. In truth, however, time is not only measured by the hands of a clock. For instance, it's been recognized that animals do not live with a sense of time. Animals have no concept of time. And in certain regions of the world, there are large communities of people, such as Native Americans and peoples of the South Pacific, who perceive time differently from the rest of us. It appears that they make no distinctions between the past, present, and future tenses in their conversations. It is a concept they don't seem to have, their thoughts always being in the present moment.

So, since they of course don't use clocks and calendars, they refer to events in nature to indicate the future, using such expressions as, "at the time of the rice harvests," "at the birth of the kittens," "when the birds lay their eggs," or "when so-and-so reaches maturity." This seems to be their form of the "future tense" in their languages. And also because they do not have a way of measuring the time of day, they determine when to meet each other by noting the location and adding expressions to say things like, "when the sun rises above that mountain," "when the sun crosses over to that field," or "when the sun travels over here to this spot." Because their thoughts always remain in the present, nature determines their sense of time. This is the shape that their "future tense" is said to take. Even now, dotted throughout the world, there are people using this type of grammar to communicate with one another.

Then what would be their form of the past tense? As with their "future tense," when they want to point to a definite time in the past, they may refer to a particular event, such as "the time that so-and-so's child was born" or "the day of so-and-so's wedding." Other than that, they speak in the present tense.

If we never received an education, we, too, may never have thought of using the past, present, and future tenses, and may naturally have referred to our natural surroundings. We would have naturally learned to speak only in the present tense. But of course, most of us have been educated to think according to the hands of the clock. We were also taught to use calendars. For example, we have been trained to think in terms of the year of our graduation or the year we began working for our current employer. And then gradually, we were ingrained with the notion that time is determined by the hands of the clock. In other words, we came to believe that time passes equally for everyone, because the clock came to determine our sense of time.

Since one hour on your clock seems the same as one hour on everyone else's clocks, you are apt to think of that one hour in your life and one hour in others' lives are created equal. But there is a huge mistake in this understanding of time. Time is difficult to perceive with the senses that we human beings have been granted since birth. The truth is, our measure of time is the sum total of our individually unique experiences and what we sense through our physical senses. Therefore, whether time feels long-lasting or brief completely depends on how each person sees it. What I mean to say is that people don't experience time equally; your experience of time depends on how you, yourself, feel, sense, and perceive it. This is actually the most natural way to experience time.

So to form a basic premise of time, please begin by questioning commonly held perceptions. Please start by questioning the notion that time is measured by clocks and is experienced similarly by everyone. Instead, please think of time as measured subjectively by the mind of each individual person. When you begin thinking of time in this way, you may notice something interesting. Everyone is given twenty-four hours in a day, without exception. But when you look back on each individual day, you might get a strange feeling; you might wonder whether each day has truly contained the same amount of time. Some days seem to have flown by so quickly that you can't even remember them, and other days have left a deep impression on your heart. So you cannot help but wonder what this could mean. This means, perhaps, that time holds a different meaning when we experience it within our minds.

When you begin to think in this way, you will see that time is not something to be measured only by the clock; time contains much more meaning and value than that. Time that can be measured by the clock is the same for everyone, so it has no detectable value. Put another way, this clock-based way of measuring time doesn't tell us anything about time's value or lack of value. But time as it is sensed within each person holds actual worth. What I am trying to say is that time should not be measured linearly, in a straight line, as we would measure something using a yardstick. Instead, when you begin to think of time as holding a certain value, as having a certain "volume," the way you see the world will change enormously. This way of understanding time can lead to changing your life in tremendous ways.

But before I move ahead in this discussion, there is still the premise of the twenty-four hours in a day that we are given equally. As people who live with clocks in our lives, we can't deny this reality. Even though it's often said that as human beings we all are born equal, we still see differences in physical appearance, income, worldly status, and gender. So there are actually many ways that we were not created perfectly equal. But if there were just one way we were all equal, it would be the twenty-four hours that we live with every day, each day of our lives. Put another way, the basic premise is that every person is equal in terms of the time that a clock can measure. And from there on, what we have to think about is how we will experience in our minds this measurable time. In other words, the issue becomes how we will change our measurable time to spiritual time—our own inner time, or time as we perceive it in our inner world.

2

TIME THAT GENERATES VALUE

As I mentioned earlier, it is true, indeed, that twenty-four hours are granted equally to everyone each day, without any exceptions. There is no doubt that you and I are given the same twenty-four hours a day according to the external, clock-based notion of time. And as they say, time can be neither added to nor subtracted from. It's impossible to use tomorrow's hours in advance or carry over yesterday's hours to use today. We can't put time into a bank account, as we do with money to build our savings, and neither can we withdraw it ahead of time, as we do when we take out a loan. These are principles that work with money. We can use the money left over from the past or that we've saved up over time and put it to use in the present. We can also spend the income we are expecting to receive at the end of this month to make purchases by credit. But even though we perceive money as working this way, this is not how we generally think time works.

But I can't help but wonder whether this is true. They often say that time is money; if that's true, then shouldn't the principles that govern money also work for time? Perhaps it doesn't work that way for the clock-based notion of time, but

I can't help but think that this may be different in the case of subjective time, the kind of time that holds worth and value.

Let me give you an example. When I, as the president of Happy Science, give a lecture in a provincial city in Japan, I usually have an average audience of ten thousand people. But suppose I were a regular office worker who came up with the concept of "living in eternity now," a subject I could talk about for an hour. I would want to present my ideas to someone. If I were a regular office worker, I would not be able to attract an audience, so I would probably invite a friend to listen to me. After listening to my one-hour talk, my friend would get some impression of my ideas and make an assessment. If we were in a coffee shop, he might treat me to a cup of coffee if he thought my words were worth the value of one. That means that one hour of my time would have generated a value of about three hundred yen. If my friend thought that my talk was worth more than that, he might invite me to a meal with him, in which case my time would have generated one thousand to two thousand yen of value. If I managed to impress him further, he might invite me for a drink, as well; my talk would then have generated about ten thousand yen of value. The results would be different according to circumstances, depending on who listened to my talk, of course. But at least in these terms, talking to one person would generate only about one thousand yen or perhaps ten thousand yen at the most. But in reality, I am able to give a lecture on the theme "Living in Eternity Now" to an audience of ten thousand people.

This encourages me to think. At my current age, and if I did not have this current role, I might have spoken to just one person, and my hour might have had an economic value of ten thousand yen at best. But by giving a lecture, I am able to talk to ten thousand people simultaneously in just one clock-based hour. So what does it mean to have an audience of ten thousand people? If I were an ordinary office worker, I would have had to give the same one-hour talk ten thousand times, once to each person in the audience, to have the same economic effect as one lecture I give today.

Comparing these two possibilities, I find that the value of an hour of my time is indeed one hour, but at the same time, it is not just the value of a single hour. Mathematically, the value of one hour as the president of Happy Science discussing the subject of "Living in Eternity Now" is equivalent to at least ten thousand of my hours if I were the average office worker. What does this mean? Someone once likened time to gold coins and said that everyone starts each morning with twenty-four gold coins. According to this metaphor, each coin remains unchanged. But in the case I have just talked about, a single golden coin has multiplied into ten thousand coins before we know it. This is a truly mystical thing. If I opened a private "Okawa Bank" and told people that if they deposited one gold coin to my bank, it would be multiplied ten thousand times in one hour, I would be flooded with customers. I'm certain about that. It may sound mysterious, but when you think of time in this way, you start to understand that the value of one hour can vary.

Let me expand on this example. Although I have an audience of ten thousand people who can actually attend my lecture on "Living in Eternity Now," there are many more who wish to listen. Not all our members around the country have the chance to attend my lecture. If I tried to satisfy the needs of these members in the usual way, I would have to give identical lectures dozens of times in different locations. How long would that take me to do? If one lecture takes one hour, then the total amount of time required would be scores of hours. But I would also have to go to each location at least one day ahead of time, so a one-hour lecture would actually involve at least two days of my time. To give dozens of lectures would take me weeks.

However, my lecture is broadcast by satellite to many other locations around the country, allowing many people to listen at once. Also, the lecture is recorded and will be made into cassette tapes* and sold. Those who miss the opportunity of attending can still listen to my lectures, even if they cannot be there in person. My lectures are also published as booklets and books for those who cannot listen to the recordings.

---

* The cassette tape was a popular medium for audio recording and replay until the early 1990s.

Thanks to these arrangements, I do not need to spend more than two days meeting the needs of my potential audience, although under normal circumstances it would take several weeks. What has happened to the rest of those days? I have actually "earned" these days and can "save" them, if I liken time to money. At first, one hour was multiplied by ten thousand, and then by tens of times more; that means an hour of my time has been expanded by hundreds of thousands of times.

As you can now see, time actually can be earned, just like money. In this example, I can reduce what would normally take several weeks to just two days, so that means I have created additional free time. I have, in fact, increased my time, and I can use this time for other purposes.

3

INVENTIONS AND INVESTMENTS TO INCREASE TIME

How did one hour expand to ten thousand hours or even hundreds of thousands of hours? I would like to think about how this happened. If an office worker can draw an audience of one listener at the very most, then how is it that my lectures can draw ten thousand listeners and enable me to expand an hour of my time ten thousandfold? I've found that two inventions underlie this phenomenon.

The first invention was to give lectures of my teachings to the world with an intention to eventually publish them. By publishing them as books, I was able to bring my teachings to the world. If I were just an author, I could get perhaps a thousand people to come to my lectures—but then it would be impossible to grow my audience further. An audience of a thousand is the best I could have done as an author, and normally authors are only able to draw audiences of three hundred, or perhaps five hundred or six hundred people at the most. So since a thousand people is the largest possible size of an author's audience, how is it that I've been able to draw tens of thousands of people to my lectures? A second invention has made this possible, and that invention was the founding of the organization called Happy Science. As an author, I was limited to audiences of a thousand people, but building this organization has enabled ten thousand people to come to my lectures.

In this way, I came up with, first, the invention of presenting my teachings to the world and, second, the invention of founding the organization. These two inventions have allowed one hour's worth of public speaking to increase ten thousandfold. And this number has increased many times more owing to the live satellite broadcasting of my lectures to many locations and the later production of cassette tapes, books, and booklets of my lectures. With time, I will see this number increase even further, expanding one hour's worth of my time infinitely. This was made possible by those two inventions or ideas I came up with previously.

Once I had come up with the idea of presenting my teachings to people and putting myself out into the world, what essential things did I need to do to turn that idea into reality? The first thing I needed to do was study. To have the kind of teachings I could put out into the world, I no doubt required a certain degree of study. I couldn't have accomplished something like that if my scope of study had been similar to that of everyday people. It went without saying, therefore, that my studies had to surpass those of everyday people.

At the same time, however, this didn't mean that I required infinite study. Suppose that ten thousand hours is required before publishing a book. Spending that length of time studying can be likened to a factory investing in new machinery. Like the factory's investment in machinery, if you knew that your "capital investment" of ten thousand hours of study would result in each of your subsequent hours being multiplied by ten thousand, then you and everyone else would rush to make that investment. If investing ten thousand hours of your time in study would let you increase one hour of your time into ten thousand hours or even hundreds of thousands of hours, then it would be obvious to anyone how worthwhile that investment would be. In this way, investing your time now can create more time for you in the future.

Next, how did the organization, Happy Science, come about? Of course, there was my original idea to create it, but that was not everything. My prior experience as a company employee became an essential source of lessons. And this experience was also a finite one. The finite length of time I spent working for a company turned out to be a kind of investment; within this defined period, I put forth effort to learn about running an organization. As a result of that effort, I was later able to think of inventing Happy Science and then make use of those lessons to manage this organization.

When I give lectures around the country, I usually attract audiences of ten thousand people wherever they are held, even if those venues are in more remote, provincial areas, such as Nagoya, Kyushu, Chugoku, Hokkaido, or Tohoku. How have I made this possible? Because I think in my mind about expanding my time. By holding the intention to increase one hour of my time by ten thousand or a hundred thousand, I manifest that intention into reality. I first hold this intention in my mind, and it is that intention that turns into reality. In other words, time can be increased, and you need to begin by understanding this concept and holding it in your mind.

Karl Marx, the economist and author of *Das Kapital* who lived more than a century ago, failed to understand this. He thought that value was produced by the hours of a person's labor and that everyone's eight hours of daily labor produced the same, equal value. Said another way, he believed that value was produced by hours of labor and that everyone basically yields the same set amount of value each hour.

But a number of wealthy people were earning a great fortune without that kind of labor. When Marx saw members of the wealthy class and the bourgeoisie collecting profits but doing so without any particular toil, Marx concluded that they were stealing the eight hours of the laborers' work. It was his view that the laborers' eight hours of work contained that many hours of value, so when he saw that labor being used by the non-laboring people working in higher positions, he saw that as an act of theft. They were stealing one, two, or as many as five hours of the laborers' hard work, in his perspective, and laborers were suffering from huge exploitation, a condition that they should not tolerate. So he felt that the laborers must fight against the exploiting class.

This was a huge misunderstanding, however. Marx's conception of time was the same notion of clock-based time that I discussed at the beginning of this chapter. One hour equals one hour for everyone, in his belief, and everyone's one hour produces the same value of output, regardless of who that person is. In comparison, the conception of time I am discussing is different; time contains value in and of itself. I believe that time contains value that can be increased and decreased and that when it is properly invested and managed, it can be increased almost infinitely, like a bank deposit that yields interest. When we consider time in this way, even though I brought up the phrase "time is money" a little earlier, we can see that time may have much more value than money. For as long as we have time, there is all sorts of work we can accomplish, and this work we do no doubt creates value. We are all given 365 days a year, and we share this same clock-based time equally, but if someone can increase his or her one year into ten years, it's clear that this would yield an economic effect that's ten times greater. Even in an administrative type of job, if ten years' worth of work could be completed in the period of a year, the work would no doubt lead to ten times the economic results. As a matter of fact, the actual produced effects will come out to be even greater than that, because the work that we do is not limited to simple and routine administrative work; it also includes advanced work. The higher the level of work, the larger the return it produces. Just as good investments of money will yield high returns, investing time well will enhance its value.

4

INCREASING THE DENSITY OF TIME

I would like to think more deeply about increasing one's time. In the chapter called "Making the Most of the Gift of Time" in my book *The Heart of Work**, I talked about the Pareto principle. This theory was developed by the Italian economist Vilfredo Pareto. As a result of his studies, he realized that everything can be divided by a ratio of 80:20. He proposed that when there is 100 percent of a project to be completed, managing just 20 percent of that total amount of work will yield a result similar to doing 80 percent of that work. When applied to a company of one hundred employees, this concept says that 80 percent of the value that a company produces is created by 20 percent of its people. This is the principle Pareto discovered. When things were divided into parts, he found that the 80:20 ratio described everything, and from this discovery, he derived the concept that you can control 80 percent of that by handling the important 20 percent.

Let us look at this idea more deeply. What does it mean, exactly? Suppose we are given the task of shoveling coal. If every worker's muscle power were equal in strength and we all

---

* Ryuho Okawa, *The Heart of Work* (New York: IRH Press, 2016).

put the same amount of effort into the ten hours of work, the amount of daily labor we produced would be equal. Not all jobs are composed of monotonous tasks, however, and most people's days consist of a range of different tasks. This holds true whether you are an office worker or a stay-at-home wife. Both accomplish a diverse range of tasks on a daily basis.

According to the Pareto principle, if your day is made of ten working hours, you are spending two of those ten hours on the most vital tasks. And when those two hours are completed, you will have completed 80 percent of your day's work. It would take you ten hours to finish your whole day's work, but two hours is actually enough time to complete 80 percent of it. This is the point that is crucial. 100 percent of a day's work will require ten total hours to complete, but it is a fact that 80 percent of a day's work can be condensed into just two hours.

What does this discovery make possible? A wise person recognizes the opportunity to increase his or her time. If you want to complete 100 percent of your work today, you have to devote ten hours to doing that, but if you resolve to complete 80 percent of your work instead, you will reduce the hours you spend on that job to only two. By using this method of working, you will create a way to increase your time. You can decide to spend two hours on your work, accepting 80 percent as your limit. By doing this, you can now work in units of two hours, spending each unit on a different subject. Working in this way every two hours, you will be multiplying 80 percent by five, which equals 400 percent. You will accomplish 400 percent each day or, put another way, your work will be quadrupled each day. By concentrating just on the vital 20 percent of tasks, one after another, you will be able to quadruple your time.

How can we put this theory into practice? Here, the idea of sharing the work comes in. For example, every company has a structure of managers and staff. The reason behind this is that it allows the manager to increase his or her time. Let me explain. Out of the ten hours it would take a manager to complete his or her job all by oneself, by finishing 20 percent of the most important work in the morning, this will result in finishing 80 percent of the work in terms of value. Then, by delegating the remaining eight hours of work to one's subordinates, this opens up eight hours of the manager's time. The manager can then use two hours from this new time toward completing another 20 percent of high-value work, which can fulfill another 80 percent of work with value. The remaining work can again, be passed down to subordinates. In this way, the manager's time will be increased fourfold, and this allows him or her to accomplish 400 percent of work with high value. This is very important; a manager's time can be expanded fourfold if he or she works with a subordinate and the subordinate is, in fact, doing not only simple tasks like shoveling coal, but also tasks that require a high level of decision-making ability.

Instead of doing all the tasks himself, the president delegates some of the tasks to the managing director, who, in turn, does the crucial 20 percent of them and then delegates

80 percent to his or her own subordinates. They, in turn, assign some of their tasks to their own assistants. If the same process is repeated at each level, how much time will be created? If you are good at mathematics, you can calculate the amount. By repeating this process, time is quadrupled at each level and can be expanded infinitely.

Now, here is the most important point. You may come across a mom-and-pop candy shop that has been in the family for generations. If the hundred-year-old shop is well managed, that is a good thing, but you can be certain that time is not being created. This applies to not only to candy shops, but also all small businesses, including grocery stores and retailers. However, there are private retailers that have expanded into big businesses with annual sales of a trillion yen within thirty years. The distribution industry provides many examples of small retailers that have turned into giant enterprises.

The secret lies in the creation of time using this principle I have just talked about. The owners of these big businesses could not have achieved this expansion single-handedly; instead, by employing efficient personnel, they have been continuously creating time. They gave other personnel the work that they, themselves, were originally thinking of working on. By creating vast amounts of time in this way, their businesses developed into huge enterprises. The idea of creating time has enabled private businesses with annual sales of less than one hundred million yen to transform into giant enterprises making one trillion yen by employing many people.

Actually, what is being produced is time. If the annual sales of a business are one hundred million yen, then it will take ten thousand years to reach sales of one trillion yen. However, businesses can actually make that amount in a year. It is incredible but true. Anyone who is successful in this world has created time, and successful people know that time is more valuable than money. If you deposit money in a bank, it yields only a small amount of interest, but time can produce a much greater yield. This idea is vital.

This is how the process of creating time works, though it often goes unnoticed. An infinite amount of time can be created, as I have explained, by entrusting tasks to others where possible, while you concentrate on the vital 20 percent of a job. If you train others so that you can further delegate tasks, you'll increase your time infinitely and the "density" of your time will increase considerably. This corresponds to what I said at the beginning: one hour of my time can be expanded to ten thousand or even hundreds of thousands of hours.

What has been done to increase the density of my time? Of course, there are people engaged in publishing booklets, books, and cassette tapes of my lectures. With their help, I can increase my time by hundreds of thousands of times. This perspective of how we use time is one type of universal principle. If you can successfully increase the density of your time, you can become a person with a wealth of time. I would like you to explore this possibility.

5

Increasing the Area of Time

In addition to the "density" or "depth" of time that I have just described, there is another important aspect of time to consider: its "area." You have probably never thought about increasing or expanding the area of your time. Actually, time has an area. If you spend ten active hours of the day doing just one thing, it's like spending all those areas facing one wall. The area of your time during those hours will be limited to that one wall. But if you turn to face different directions over the course of the day, you'll be able to see at least four walls. What I am pointing out has to do with how you direct your attention over the course of a day. If you change the direction you're facing three times, you can face four different walls, which means that you will quadruple the area of your time. This metaphor of a room is just one illustration; if you experiment, you will find various ways of enlarging the area of your time.

This metaphor shows that in the same day, you can perform a variety of different types of work, study, and attend to other activities. This is the way to increase the area of your time. Let me explain this differently. I mentioned earlier that you can accomplish 80 percent of your vital work by working on it for two hours out of ten during a day. This lets you condense ten hours into two, which leaves you with eight remaining hours. If you spend all eight hours on the same domain of work, you will multiply your work productivity by five. But what happens if you shift the domain of your work every two hours? You'll see a different outcome.

There are multitalented people in the world who are involved in many different fields of activity. They may write books, manage businesses, appear on TV, perform music, and travel extensively. Their work is truly multifaceted. Perhaps they are a mystery to you, and you may think that they were born with a wide range of talents. This is certainly true in a sense, but talent alone cannot explain the diversity of their activities. Those multitalented people are examples of people who increased the area of their time in the way I have just explained.

Productivity cannot be greatly enhanced by doing just one thing, even if the density of time is increased. By allotting each unit of two hours to a different activity, you can work in a variety of fields, and that will allow you to reap greater results for the time you invest. Suppose there is an office worker who is a company man, and another office worker with similar abilities who spends an hour a day reading. The fruits of this reading will become apparent in three, five, or ten years' time, when this office worker will have achieved a certain depth of cultivation. Although his colleague may continue to do the same job without making any changes, the person who has been reading for an hour every day will, in five years, have acquired enough depth of knowledge to fulfill different responsibilities. He will have become an expert in another field, and after five more years, he will become an even superior one.

That's an example of someone who reads for an hour every day. Suppose there is a third person who spends one hour reading and another hour pursuing an artistic activity, such as playing the piano, the violin, singing, or listening to music. Ten years of this activity will produce significant results in the arts. Having cultivated considerable ability, even as an amateur, this person will have become very capable in that field. In this way, you can extend your horizons into various artistic arenas. You can also widen your circle of friends, and your new friends may bring you new work opportunities. You may meet someone who says, "You seem very versed in music, would you like to join our association?" "We perform on stage, and we'd be glad if you can join us," "Can you be our coordinator?" or, "You should consider going professional." These invitations will open doors to various opportunities, and they are examples of what can happen if you spend an hour each day reading and practicing music.

Other people may expand their activities with hobbies, such as Japanese chess, the game of Go, or travel; still others may take up a physical activity such as tennis, swimming, or just ten minutes of exercise a day. These people are incorporating a variety of activities into their lives, giving their time a greater "area," and in the future, this will widen their horizons. With a broader range of activities, they will have a wider world to live in. Instead of mixing only with colleagues from their own division at work, they will come into contact with people from many different walks of life. Consequently, they may achieve things that are not possible for a regular office worker engaged only in his or her work.

For instance, if you join a sport or a gym, you may make friends with people from various other fields. For example, you might meet the presidents or general managers of other companies. Five years on, you may come across a task related to this sport or to a fellow club member's line of business. You may wonder if you could ask a favor of one of those presidents and decide to give him or her a call. He or she may well answer, "Ah, it's you! I can certainly take care of that for you." In a case like this, a telephone conversation of two or three minutes could win you a contract that would be hardly possible to settle even in a year, and you may consequently get a speedy promotion.

In this way, you are increasing your time and enabling your success by getting involved in different fields of activity. Expanding the area of time will lead you to cultivate new areas of interest that provide you more opportunities to create time. Although everyone is living the same twenty-four hours a day, each of us lives in a completely different world, depending on the depth and area of our time.

6

THE VOLUME OF TIME, THE SUM TOTAL OF A LIFE

What happens, then, when we multiply the "density" (or depth, or even height) of time by the "area" of time? We get the three-dimensional "volume" of time. The volume of time is the end result of how you have lived a lifetime of eighty years. From the viewpoint of the theory of time, the volume of time ("density" times "area") amounts to the sum total of your life. What is important is how much time you have created in your life—not the length of time, but the volume.

Those who have achieved a lot in this world have created a large amount of time over the course of their lives. Others, who have been unsuccessful, have spent very monotonous lives made up of time as it's measured by the clock's hands or the days on a calendar. The eighty years of life of someone who has accomplished a great deal can be worth more than eighty years. That person may have expanded eighty years into eight hundred years, two thousand years, or even ten thousand years. Understanding this is an extremely important part of living a life of victory.

7

BUDGETING TIME:
TURNING TIME INTO GOLD

I hope that the idea of the density and area of time is becoming clear to you. I have talked about things that most people can understand. Now, let me take this opportunity to talk about some things that lie beyond those subjects.

Happy Science teaches the objective and mission of life. The objective of life is for our souls to gain many different experiences by being reborn into this world. We come to this world and leave it for the other world through the process of reincarnation. The mission of your life is to make your soul shine and help create utopia on Earth. I think that when you consider these things from the viewpoint of the theory of time that I have just explained, you may realize something about the purpose and mission of life. Those who have aims or goals and have an image of the path to be taken can complete their work smoothly. Others who do not have any image of the future and are unsure of which way to go have to repeat a process of trial and error. They let a lot of time go to waste. But those who have a clear understanding of the objective and mission of life can avoid wasting time.

Let me explain the objective and mission of life in a simpler way. A human being is a spiritual being—in other words, a child of God. The essential nature of a child of God is to actualize one's mission in this world. What is the mission of children of God? It is to turn this earthly world, which is the training ground of souls, into a utopia. What is a utopian society like? It is a world where everyone on Earth can live well and love each other. It is a world filled with light. We incarnate into this world with such a mission to manifest an ideal world on Earth. Once you are aware of this, how does it affect the way of your life? It dramatically reduces the time you waste, compared with those who have to go through a process of trial and error.

Some who read this book may be skeptical about the existence of the other world, but it exists, 100 percent. I can affirm this from my own experience. There is no room in me for any doubt, because I have confirmed through my own experience that the other world really exists. It cannot be a fact that's 99 percent true. It must be 100 percent true. What exists, exists; there is no means of denying it. Those who have had no experience of the other world may not be able to understand it, but it is an undeniable fact to those who have.

What I want to say, in asserting that the other world definitely exists, is that there is a great difference between the person who realizes this fact after death and the person who knows it while still alive. The former will let a considerable amount of time go to waste in his or her earthly life. If you are made aware of this fact early on in your life, you can lessen the time you waste. In other words, you can manage your time. As I explained earlier, you can maximize the density and area of your time to accomplish your life's great task.

In this way, time is much more valuable than money, so you have to determine how you will use your time, just as you learn to budget money. You need to decide how you want to spend your time, just as you decide how you want to spend your money. Just as a budget consists of different uses of money, you must also determine the uses for your time and how to use your time most effectively. This will help you increase the density of your time. In addition, you need to increase the area of time. During your lifetime, it's necessary to maximize both the density and the area of your time. Budgeting time is of crucial importance. One day is limited to twenty-four hours, and an average lifetime is about eighty years, so it is particularly important to allocate this limited time to what is essential so that you can create as much time as possible.

We talk about various things related to the spiritual world. Spiritual phenomena occur, and spiritual messages are published. I believe our activities have caused many people to become interested in the other world. It is a good thing to be interested, and studying Happy Science's teachings will make all these things quite natural. It's natural to us that the other world exists, that there are guardian and guiding spirits, and that Heaven and Hell exist in the other world.

But no matter how much spiritual knowledge you have, you are living in this world, not the other world. In German, we who live here on Earth are described as "Dasein": beings who live here and now. Living here and now means that we are existences containing time. What then, must we, as Dasein, do? We should live in a way that will make the most of the time we have here in this world. To do this you need to know both the existence of the spiritual world and your life's mission. But, most importantly, you should make your life shine with the greatest brilliance and turn your time on Earth to gold.

No matter how much interest you have in the spiritual world, you must start from making the most of your time in this world, combusting your life's energy to the fullest. Time consists of separate days, and your mission in life is to turn each day into gold. You must not use your knowledge of the other world as a refuge from this world. Instead, make each day worthwhile and fill your days with golden light.

The more you come to know about the Truths, the more I would like you to appreciate the value of time, cherish each day of your life, and live every day as if it were an entire lifetime. This is vital. The more deeply you study the Truths, I would like you to live a better life, cherish your time, turn your time into pure gold, and treat each day with great care instead of wasting it. Please cherish your gold coins instead of throwing them into a ditch. Increase their number, and spend them for others' benefit. This is my sincere wish.

This is the meaning of "living in eternity now." You should not be interested solely in the other world, for our life essentially contains the time of now. So value your time now—otherwise you cannot say that you are exploring the Truths in the right way. To explore the Right Mind is to explore, find, and create time in the right way. I hope you will take this opportunity to think about the meaning of time once again.

CHAPTER FIVE

THE PATH TO HUMAN COMPLETION

1

A Journey of Eternal Hopes and Ideals

The theme that I have chosen for this chapter is, "The Path to Human Completion." Being such a vast theme, I wouldn't be able to end this discussion in this chapter alone, so in this chapter, I will provide you an invitation to entering the path to human completion.

The number of books I have put out into the world is now more than one hundred titles.* You may have read a number of them from various angles, but the full picture of what Happy Science does and teaches may have been difficult to grasp. In simple words, our philosophy aims to create many outstanding people to bring changes to the modern world. Said briefly, my teachings are in the tradition of Shakyamuni Buddha, who preached in India 2,600 years ago to create enlightened, awakened people. It was the same with Confucius, who, 2,500 years ago in China, constantly taught the path of the virtuous leader. I am not encouraging people of these present times to become that kind of traditional leader, but my teachings include the

---

* As of 1993, the publication date of the original Japanese edition. As of November 2019, Ryuho Okawa has published more than 2,600 titles.

same essence. The path to a virtuous leader is the same as the path to human completion. For while our soul-training as a human being continues, there can be no true end to our journey or our spiritual discipline—this is the nature of this path.

I ask you to see this path as your eternal hopes and your eternal ideals. With this as your starting point, your studies at Happy Science should lead to developing into a splendid person, to good changes in you, to a growth into an ideal person in others' eyes. If your studies do not lead to changes like these, the Happy Science organization will cease to hold all meaning. Our first task is to create positive changes in each and every person. Creating miracles of the rare and extraordinary kind has not been our aim; rather, we have aimed to accomplish only the ordinary. We have wished to help many people advance one step, two steps, or three steps forward, in the most ordinary way, based on the study of my teachings; this is what my philosophy has been about. So you see that behind my way of thinking there is a highly sound and grounded philosophy.

If our purpose were simply to create miracles, I can, because I do hold the ability to perform great miracles. I am capable of accomplishing this. It has just been my preference not to, because my desire is to leave teachings for the countless people of the future, including those who will be born two or three thousand years from now. It is surely splendid to witness an age of miracles, but with the passage of time, such an age fades into mythology. The many who look back on it might think, "Perhaps there used to be a time like that, long ago. Maybe marvelous times like that truly existed before." But for the most part, they regard an age of miracles as fictional tales and made-up fantasies. They look on such an age as unrelated to the times they live in.

So my messages are not confined to people only in this current age. I also want to offer the chance for human completion to those who will come five hundred, a thousand, and two thousand years in the future; this is what I have wished to do. I am taking an approach that is steady and simple for this reason, even though I am capable of far more mystical messages and actions. At Happy Science, I place great emphasis on studying the Truths while we live in these times together. A movement like this would ordinarily emerge after I'm gone from this earthly world. I have already started it by giving lectures, however, because I don't want to divert the path of Truths and I want my thinking to be imparted to many people from the start.

2

THE BURNING DESIRE
OF YOUR SOUL

In every age, there have been people who sought the Truths from their own depths. Behind this is a spiritual truth that they were born to Earth, as a group, with a mission. We are not born in different ages separately, expecting to seek the path individually. In every age was always a group of people who've emerged on Earth to create the spirit of that age.

I would like to tell everyone who reads this book about the difficulty of being born into this world, in this present era. Numerous opportunities to do so have been available to you over the past several hundred years, and you will see more opportunities in the times to come. But this place and this era were where you chose to be born. To make this choice, you must have known for a fact that many other people were also being born on Earth in this age to build the new spirit of the times. You were aware of this, and you could not do otherwise than be born onto Earth in these same times.

Look into the depths of your soul and ask this question: could it have been by coincidence that you were born in this very place in this very era? This was probably not the case.

Inside you, there must have been a very, very strong desire to be born. You must have gone to the greatest lengths to be born in this place, at this time. Perhaps this sounds like an easy task to accomplish. But to have been born into this time, during the makings of extraordinary heights in human history, is itself a difficult thing.

So do not let yourself forget how tremendous are the expectations you bear and how great is the hope you shoulder for future generations. Your spiritual training will be in vain if you remain unaware of the meaning of this current era and a sense of mission in your life. Without this awareness, whatever you may study may come to no avail. You must not forget that your existence in this age, the very fact that you are here, is your burning desire manifested. You mustn't forget that your existence in this present era is the manifestation of thousands of years of your soul's burning desire.

You may believe that you picked up this book through your own will. But there has been a being who led you to it. Perhaps this was invisible and physically unrecognizable, but this world we live in is more than we can see with our eyes, hear through our ears, and touch with our hands. To those who live in Heaven, the third-dimensional, phenomenal world appears as if through a fishbowl. Through the eyes of the higher world, the third dimension is like a fishbowl atop a desk, and all the people are swimming goldfish; this is the way our existence appears to them. If the goldfish jump out of the fishbowl, they will perish, and for this reason, they need to stay within the fishbowl's bounds, even though it may restrict their freedom. I would like to help everyone see that this is what our existence at the present time is like.

3

Your Guardian Spirit Is Standing Beside You

Surrounded by such a world, it seems you are swimming in complete freedom. But when you find something of higher value, resolve to pursue higher ideals, and guide your will in that direction, other beings are definitely there, encouraging you. These beings are your guardian spirits, which you may often have heard me talk about. Your guardian spirit is not a stranger to you at all. He or she is actually a part of your own soul. Perhaps that may not be something you've heard said before. Perhaps it sounds unfamiliar to your ears. Perhaps you are skeptical. But if I were to reveal the meaning of your true existence, you'd see that you, who was born into this world and is dwelling in your physical body does not represent the whole of you. Your soul is a much greater being of much greater energy and wisdom.

You have probably heard about the subconscious mind. We are often informed of the conscious mind and the subconscious mind and that we ordinarily use the former to contemplate decisions and guide our actions. It's true. But even though you may be living in this way, there are times when an idea you did not expect suddenly comes up. It might be about the course of your life or a new job, or when you're contemplating during life's crossroads about whether to move forward, backward, left, or right. In these moments, such ideas and words well up suddenly, out of nowhere and out of context. They well up from the depths of your heart, or they may seem to fall from above. Sometimes they appear in someone else's words. One day, someone may speak the exact words you needed to hear. These occurrences show that you are not alone at all in this life, even if it seems that way.

There is a being who is supporting you and standing by you throughout your life. There is an infinite power hidden within your subconscious mind. Within everyone's souls are several soul siblings who exist in the world beyond this world. Among these beings, one is guiding you as your guardian spirit, the being best suited to give you advice to fulfill your mission. This being may be the one who will be born onto Earth in your next incarnation, or he or she may be your most recent past life. In this way, you are being protected by the being who is best suited to help you in this life and offer you guidance. When you realize the existence of such a guiding being, you will awaken to the fact that your life holds a great responsibility.

4

THE ACHIEVEMENT IS NOT MINE ALONE

On the topic of human completion, many people are living on the surface of their lives. If you were to approach each person, you would probably discover that nearly everyone has been concerned about how people think of them. They have been depicting their ideal selves through the lens of others' perspectives. You would see just how common that this is. But measuring one's success from the point of view of others is not an ideal state of mind to constantly have; it is so important to become aware of this fact. A countless number of people are spending their whole lives in this state of mind. In fact, the higher the status and worldly position one has been able to achieve, the more likely it is that other people's opinions and perspectives have been, time after time, one's source of self-assessment. I believe that this is likely to be true anywhere you look, for example, in the world of politics, business, or academia.

Those who measure themselves against external values are far from human completion. This is because they do not know the deep truths about human life. Perhaps it cannot be seen with our eyes—perhaps we are ordinarily unable to sense its existence—but a world exists from which we are constantly receiving many things; such is our human existence. We human beings are constantly being guided by many beings. These beings are always guiding us toward opportunities and leading us toward various encounters with people and life's destinies. They are constantly supplying us with such things. You may be living in this third-dimensional world freely and following the whims of your wishes while never realizing that. If you depart from this world like this, feeling satisfied at the end of your life, then you're mistaken. In truth, we cannot accomplish anything through our efforts alone.

Since I have mainly taught about self-discipline and self-effort, it may seem unusual that I say this, but we, human beings, in this world cannot truly succeed at or accomplish anything through solely our own power. This fact is something we need to always bear in mind. And why is it that we can do nothing on our own? Even if we disregard the other spiritual world, there is always the existence of other people when we try to accomplish something in this world. Perhaps other people will have given you their help actively, or maybe it will have been passively, or perhaps they will have opposed you. But as we human beings progress through our lives, each idea and action is always manifested through other people's influence. Each is an outcome of other people's existence, reactions, thoughts, and actions.

So when you look back at the journey you have taken thus far, if you can only remember how well you've done for yourself, then there is something you have forgotten. In fact, there are many things that you have overlooked. You've been putting in your effort—that's probably true—but your efforts were made possible because of the people around you. Other people have fostered the circumstances that helped manifest them. Even if you were a person of extraordinary ability, you wouldn't be able to accomplish much at all if everyone were to impede your self-realization. I have given numerous lectures, for example, but I couldn't have accomplished this through my will alone. I am able to give lectures because there are people who help me prepare them and others who are willing to listen. It may seem as though anything can be accomplished through one's will, but please don't forget that there are always essential conditions that depend on other people's existence.

The many people you admire may seem to have enjoyed their freedom and gone through life as they pleased, and this way of life may seem to have led them to completion. But that's not truly the case. The conditions of freedom are called by another name, and that's "responsibility." Those who have truly walked the path to completion are those who have understood this condition underlying freedom. As a result, the people who have accomplished the most are those who feel the most gratitude for others. This is because the higher your position rises and the greater the influence you gain, the stronger you'll feel that these achievements did not result from your own efforts. This is a vital starting point that I wish to earnestly, strongly emphasize. You are being given your life by a great power and through a great many other people's existence; this is a truth that's very important to accept. Unless you can accept this fact, your ideas and actions cannot truly be considered to have been a part of your growth, no matter how they are manifested.

5

THE GREAT TREE OF LIFE

From the micro-perspective of human existence, from a small vantage point, we all may seem to exist independently. But from the broader view of a macro-perspective, we can instead see humanity as one colossal tree with an endless number of roots. The main root branches out into smaller roots, which in turn branch out into greater numbers of fine, capillary-like roots.

That we branch out in this way is the real truth of our human souls. Each one of us is one of these strands of fine, hair-like roots at the ends of the larger root. What would happen if one of these roots believed that all the nutrients should go to it alone or that it alone should receive all the water? If such a thing were to happen, it would lead to the demise of this gigantic tree. And could this single tree root survive if the tree itself died? I don't think it would be able to. It is the nutrients and water that are absorbed by the tree's many other roots that allow the tree to grow larger and larger. And in being a part of this great system, we feel a burning sense of mission, power, and great joy. Please bear in mind these words when thinking about your path of completion.

We cannot forget that from the perspective of the grand universe, all of us—all human souls, as well as the souls of all the animals and plants—appear as one, as one vast tree standing singularly. From a third-dimensional perspective, all living beings may appear as separate existences. Each root and each leaf may seem to exist individually, as if each is a separate being. But from a much higher, far grander, spiritual perspective, everything appears as part of the singular tree of life. If the roots of this tree were to represent human souls, the leaves would, perhaps, represent all the plants of this world, and the fruits or the individual layers of bark may represent the animals. This is how the various parts of this tree are made up of many types of souls. Therefore, we must not forget that every living being in the grand universe exists to give life to this singular and vast tree of life.

As the tree absorbs water and nutrients, it grows. At times, it also undergoes various processes—such as transpiration, carbon fixation, and photosynthesis—so that it can continue to grow. While this tree grows, at times the leaves may wither and fall off as part of the process. There will also be times when insects gnaw at the fruits, leading them to spoil. There may be other times when the tree's bark will get scratched up, birds come to nest in the branches, or a part of the root gets torn up and dies. As you can see, there are many things that can happen to this tree, just as this world may bring inconveniences or moments when things don't seem to go quite smoothly.

But what cannot be forgotten is that the tree as a whole is striving to continue its life as it endures all these things.

6

THE PATH TO HUMAN COMPLETION

Once you can see human existence as like this metaphorical tree, what is the next thing you must do? I ask you to ponder this question. In fact, you have been given the role of an important, a most vital part of this tree of life; you are the very root. No matter how colossal the tree may be, it could not but perish if the roots didn't exist. That is why you are a key part. In fact, the root is the foundation that supports the tree's growth. This being the case, you must do the following three things.

Awakening to Your True Mission

First, I ask you to think of your true mission as offering nothing to be gained for yourself. Just as the water and nutrients are absorbed by the roots and are then carried upward to the trunk, your accomplishments may almost seem to stay with you, but it only seems that way. They will actually remain with you only for a time. You have to offer them up to something higher. There is nothing in this world—not gains, not benefits, nor anything magnificent or outstanding—to lay claim to as yours alone. I ask you to be aware of this as your basic premise.

Such things may come to you and stay for some length of time. They may pass in front of your eyes. But your attempt to stop them would mean the demise of this tree of life. This is a truth that needs to be known. When you think that these things belong to you, when you try to claim them for yourself, when you try to take them away from the tree as a whole, the great tree of life withers. This is the very first premise.

Perhaps you have heard of the place called Hell. You may now be more capable of imagining this world. Sometimes, among the people who are a part of this great tree of life, who bear the role of the tree's roots, there are people who misunderstand. There are people who insist on the freedom of the roots and seek only their own water, their own nutrients. Forgetting their original mission, forgetting who they originally were, they begin to think only of themselves, and they try to hold onto the water and nutrients. What would happen then?

They may not come to realization.
They may not ever realize.
But look up high, where the trunk is.
See the tree's branches.
See the leaves, how they wilt.
See this blossom, how nearly lifeless it is.
See that fruit, how near it is to death.
See the tree, how it has ceased to grow.
See the annual rings that no longer form.
Have you noticed these things happening?

There are always guiding spirits of light telling us these things. Since the roots living underground cannot see above the ground, they begin to think that they aren't related to what is occurring above them. Forgetting their original mission, they think that they have nothing to do with what's happening above the ground, and they try to keep the nourishment. But whether you retain the water and nutrients to yourself, containing them only within your area of the tree, or let them flow upwards, there will always be the same set store available to you. There will be no difference. But a great death awaits you and the very tree of life when you forget your mission.

The originating cause of Hell lies here. Those above ground are suffering, weakening, and nearing death, but each and every one of the roots living underground is only thinking about itself. This is why people of great character, who are known as the guiding spirits of light, always come down to this world to expound the teachings of the true law. They preach and preach and never cease until their last breath; never do they stop, even at the cost of being crucified, as Jesus Christ was.

There exists a sense of crisis, an awareness that the gigantic tree of life, constructed by all the universe, may perish unless these truths are taught. For this very reason, you are being taught your mission. For this very reason, you shouldn't think only of yourself. For this very reason, you are taught to love others, to love thy neighbors. We are always preaching not to live for the sake of yourself alone. This is the reality. Please don't let this be forgotten. Never should this fact leave your mind. This is the first point to bear in mind. I am speaking of that great sense of mission to be awakened within you. It must never leave your mind that this sense of mission is nothing novel; it is something that you have always possessed by nature. Please think of how much there is for you to accomplish now, having forgotten this mission that is within you by nature. How important this mission is right now. How important and urgent it is for modern people to realize their mission and act. This was my first point.

Freeing the Potential Within You

There is another, second, point. That is that your own work is not the only thing you should be immersed in accomplishing. I have said, just now, that as roots, our mission is to absorb the water and nutrients and carry them upwards. Could this truly be all there is for us to do? Should we simply be passing along what comes to us? A film called *Modern Times*, by Charlie Chaplin, came out a long time ago. *Modern Times* depicted a person with a humorous personality working at the simple task of tightening nuts onto the bolts that a conveyor belt carried to him. As human beings, we're apt to get buried in simple tasks like this. We take for granted that each and every day comes and rolls by, ever so ordinarily. And we are apt to set limits on ourselves, telling ourselves things like, "This is as much as I'm capable of. I'm just a root, after all. This is all I'll ever be able to amount to."

At times like these, we need to consider whether there might be a lot more work to be accomplished. What if you were to be asked, "Rather than being a root that's skinny like capillary vessels, why not seek to grow and become a bigger root? You'd be able to contribute to many more people then. In fact, maybe you could become large enough to support the whole tree. Ask yourself whether this could truly be a possibility for you." If you heard someone say this to you, would you believe that such a thing wouldn't really be possible for you? The truth is that it is.

My belief is that tremendous capability exists within human beings. I often say that we are truly capable of administrative work that is tenfold the work we are accomplishing now. But in the spiritual realm of work, the difference in capability between those who haven't yet awakened to their mission compared with those who have awakened to their mission and are putting their all into their work is not just a hundredfold or even a thousandfold, but ten thousandfold or even more. When a truly awakened person emerges, the power is not merely ten thousandfold, but a millionfold. This magnitude of power exists within you. This is the way we humans are. What would the work accomplished by a central, awakened person look like? It would be more than the work of just a single person. Spiritually accomplished work has tremendous influence and the power to spread. Spiritually awakened people have the ability to accomplish magnificent work that would normally be beyond their imagination.

Over the course of several years, I have spoken to millions of people.* If you include those who have listened to my tapes or read my books, this number increases to tens of millions of people. If I had gone about my life as an ordinary person, I could not possibly have accomplished this work, even if I had attempted to speak to large audiences. But I awakened to the mission that was given to me, and I thought that this was something I had to do, that the effort would not be for me alone, and that now that I was aware of my mission, I needed to send water and nourishment to as many people as possible. So I acted on these thoughts, and when I did, my messages reached tens of millions of people within a span of several years. I was able to tell them about the burning, flaming passion that comes from far beyond our world.

I've given lectures all around Japan, and now an audience of tens of thousands of people feels small to me. When I look out at such an audience, I see far more people spreading before me. I know that the people attending my lectures are not the only people I'm speaking to. When I travel to rural areas of the country, I deliver my lectures while imagining the entire population, the millions of people who live in the area surrounding

---

* As of November 2019, Ryuho Okawa has given more than 3,000 lectures, of which over 140 have been in English. He continues to give lectures around the world.

the venue. I do this because I believe, without a doubt, that those in the audience who came to listen to me will share the passion of my words with others. There are some rural areas that I seldom visit, but in a single visit, I give my lecture thinking of hundreds of thousands and millions of people affected by that single talk.

This is the nature of work that is accomplished through our inner spirit—or, put another way, this is the nature of spiritual work. There may be a limit to the ability of one person, but once your work becomes spiritual and is set afire, your ability becomes infinite. A single burning blade of grass doesn't produce much of a flame all by itself. But when this single blade of grass ignites into a flame, that flame will spread to others and set them alight too. When this happens, that fire will indeed come to hold powerful vigor. The flames of a burning brush can change the fate of the country. Your self-image may be that of a single blade of withered grass, but you must never forget that the flames that this grass sets alight will never be extinguished; they can know only boundlessly increasing energy.

Please take to heart this second point about the road to human completion: In the realm of spiritual work, one's ability can know no limit. Third-dimensional work can have limitations. But once you've awakened to your own mission, there can be no limitations to your work. Your mission will become a power that carries forward over hundreds and thousands of years—no, for longer than that—and that power will go beyond Japan and spread throughout the world. This is a splendid fact that you must be aware of. It is for this reason that I would like to tell you that, as the second important point in seeking human completion, you must free the innate potential lying within you. There is nothing else for you to do but release it.

Accumulating Wisdom

There is a third point I would like to tell you about. When this spiritual power is freed, it will spread like flames of wildfire. So when it does, we need to remain people of wisdom. Passion is a great energy in this world. In fact, it is a singular energy for accomplishing great work. And to enable this passion to elevate further and become even more remarkable, we need to make use of wisdom. As you spread your passion, you will have numerous experiences. And as you gain completely new experiences, they will become a part of you. They will imbue the knowledge within you with power. Wisdom is generally considered the result of experience added to knowledge.

Everyone possesses knowledge. As we read books, learn from various people, and attend school, we gain a great deal of knowledge, which continues to increase day by day. But the power of knowledge is not enough; we must not forget that. Knowledge is just the ingredients. It is true that the power of knowledge may weaken without a constant accumulation, but it is still just the ingredients. What imbues these ingredients with power is passion. And passion provides you with opportunities called experience.

We need to value the wisdom that arises from combining knowledge with passion. The person you are this year should be many times more wise than the person you were last year, and you should be many more times wiser come next year. Wisdom gives you the ability to guide a great many people in the right direction. Knowledge alone does not give you this power. Neither does passion on its own. Passion is the flame of expanding fire, but it does not move in a fixed direction. Its flames don't always spread in accord with your thoughts. But when wisdom is added, the flames of passion begin to accomplish work. This work will be constructive and positive and will improve this world in perceivable ways, accomplishing remarkable things.

So you must accumulate wisdom daily. This wisdom will become your own treasure. But sitting down and reading books is not enough for this wisdom to well up within you, nor is simply listening to other people. These activities are nothing more than ingredients, like the lead inside a furnace that turns into gold. In the right furnace, these ingredients can be transformed into pure gold. This is why, from this point on, you need to learn the Truths as a matter of course, and the Truths will go hand in hand with deeds inspired by passion, and these two things, knowledge and deeds, which can also be called knowledge and experience, will continue to produce wondrous and one-of-a-kind gems of wisdom.

The wisdom that is born will in turn accomplish great works, much like the work of a large, turning cogwheel. Without wisdom, we are only capable of using our energy in one direction. But if you could look inside a large machine, you'd see various combinations of gears directing energy in a set direction and allowing the machine to move to the right, to the left, upwards, or downwards—in many directions. This is the true way that we should be accomplishing our work. Passion alone will not help us determine a set direction. Or passion may only be able to move headlong. But when we add wisdom to passion, numerous cogwheels will guide our work in various directions, giving us the ability to have various kinds of influence in many different directions.

The Exploration of the Right Mind

I have finished laying out the three basic principles for walking on the path to human completion. The first principle is that nothing in this world can be claimed for yourself only and that you exist to serve a higher purpose. The second principle is that spiritual work accomplished through the power of passion knows no bounds. And the third principle is that when the cogwheel called wisdom gives you, the holder of this power, a direction in which to channel it, you become capable of accomplishing superior work. These three principles are the basics and the starting points. But just practicing these principles does not put you on the path to human completion. While it is necessary to constantly keep these perspectives in mind, there is also one more thing you must do: you must explore your mind.

As human beings, each of us has a mind. And in fact, it's not exactly right to say that we have a mind; it isn't a mistake to say that we have our mind only. After death, the only possession we take with us to the other world is our mind. This is all we're allowed to bring. We can't bring back our eyeglasses, our shirts, or our neckties; we can only bring our mind. Therefore, our spiritual training as human beings can only be about bettering our mind. So, in addition to having a sense of mission, you absolutely cannot forget to explore your mind. At Happy Science, we call this the Exploration of the *Right* Mind.

What is "right" is not easily recognized, however. The reason is that "right mind" has another name: "God's mind." Because it is we human beings who are exploring the world of God's mind, "righteousness" cannot be discovered uniformly; there are no bounds to our ability to understand "righteousness." However deeply we explore what "righteousness" is, we can never understand it perfectly. In truth, we are on a path of eternal improvement. And while you are on this path of exploring Right Mind, there are several vital practices that will be indispensable to your development into an exceptional human being.

The first thing you must do is refrain from holding onto negative thoughts. Negative thoughts may include, for example, wishing harm upon others or wishing harm upon yourself. They may be complaints, discontentment, jealousy, suspicion, or various other kinds of thoughts. When we think about it, there are endless kinds of negative thoughts. So you must control your mind so that you don't hold onto these negative thoughts; this is the first practice of exploring the Right Mind.

The second practice is to self-reflect promptly when negative thoughts take control of your mind and become expressed in your words or actions. If a wrong thought becomes manifested, self-reflect without delay, and then resolve to never again speak the same words or commit the same deeds. Make the effort to stop negative thoughts from manifesting outwardly, and instill in yourself the habit of immediate self-reflection when they do.

The third practice is to consistently rid yourself of the dirt that covers your mind. This is not a one-time task or a task that ends in an instant. However high your position may rise, however important a person you may become, and whatever kind of enlightenment you may attain, your mind can still develop clouds at any stage. So you must never forget that your mind is a mirror that needs to be polished continuously every day. Always bear in mind that your mind needs to be buffed and shined on a constant basis. The standing you hold in society, your status, the title of your position, or the praise you receive from others will not justify your avoiding to clean your mind. The higher a position you occupy, the more sternly you should practice self-reflection. The higher you stand above others, the more things there will be that could cloud your mirror. This is a discipline that we must practice eternally. There is no end to this discipline for human beings, and we cannot forget that while we continue on the path of this eternal practice, we are walking the path to human completion.

CHAPTER SIX

ON THE
ROYAL ROAD
OF LIFE

1

THE TRUE LEADER

In this chapter, I would like to talk about the royal road of life from the standpoint of the way to becoming a leader. The royal road of life is the path that every person who is born to this world and is leading or wants to lead others must undergo. It is very difficult for you to stand above many others and lead them in the true sense unless you take this road.

In the first chapter of this book, I taught the heavenly way of life for people whose state of mind accords with the fourth-, fifth-, and almost the sixth-dimensional worlds of Heaven, which is something we teach at Happy Science.* Now, this chapter will discuss essential soul-training for entering the upper level of the sixth dimension, called the world of light, and also for advancing further to the seventh dimension, which is the world of *bodhisattvas*, or the eighth dimension, the world of *tathagatas*. The reason is that those in the sixth dimension's upper level, who are souls referred to as *arhats*, begin to have outstanding leadership abilities, and leaders of the true sense have, at the lowest, this level of enlightenment.

---

* In the other world of Earth, the souls are divided into different realms from the fourth dimension to the ninth dimension, according to the individual's level of faith and enlightenment. See Ryuho Okawa, *The Nine Dimensions* (New York: IRH Press, 2012).

So, what are the qualities of a true leader? A true leader may no doubt hold a position of leadership of the worldly sense. However, the conditions of a leader that I am presenting here refer not merely to worldly status, but to the conditions that would be more than approved in the world of the Truths.

2

RESPECT, THE FIRST CONDITION OF A TRUE LEADER

I would like to begin with the first condition for becoming a leader. The first condition of leadership is the heart of respect.

In someone who stands at the summit of leadership, the heart of respect will manifest as nobleness of soul. It manifests as a noble atmosphere, character, and aura. But many reading this book are probably in their progress of becoming true leaders. What does the heart of respect mean for them? One way it manifests in them is through their dignity, and an additional way is through their politeness of conduct.

Some will no doubt question these conditions of leadership. So I will explain the reason. To understand the royal road, one must also understand the road of "the rule of might," the path that is directly opposed to the royal road. Those who follow the rule of might may attain high status in the worldly sense and be exceptional people and highly talented. But they are lacking in two characteristics. One of these characteristics is the fragrance of dignity. Said another way, they don't have respectable dignity, and their soul-tendency is heading in the wrong direction. Therefore, dignity is the first gate which must be passed through. Those with the wrong character have not yet earned acceptance onto the royal road.

What does dignity refer to? I would require endless words on this subject, but if you are ever to enter the royal road, you must feel unashamed of having your mind seen into, being discovered for who you truly are, and having your inner being displayed in front of others' eyes. If you cannot bear to lay bare your thoughts, words, and actions, however you conceal them, they clearly demonstrate lesser dignity.

Another characteristic of those following the rule of might is an absence of politeness and respectfulness. Everywhere we look, there are very capable achievers. But some of the achievers on the path of "might is right" do not respect people who are above them in some way, their superiors, and other outstanding people. They not only carelessly mock, scorn, and refuse to respect the strong; they also slander them in the shadows; such is the heart that lacks respect. Those with this heart are on the path of the rule of might.

Perhaps many think of themselves as members of the elite. But I ask you to bring stillness to your mind and reflect quietly. Ask yourself, have you been taking the royal road or the path of might is right? For those on the path of might is right, however high the position or however great the fame you have attained in this world, there is sure ruin awaiting you, whether in this world on Earth or in the afterlife. That you realize this is so vital to you.

Those among the outstanding,
Those of extraordinary qualities beyond others,
Let not the heart of respect be forgotten,
For when you allow it to,
Your extraordinariness ceases to hold the light of God.
As you forget the heart of respect,
So shall you sink into the way of might is right.
You must let the heart of respect be your starting point.

When, in time,
Up the ladder of success you climb,
Over ten, twenty, or thirty years,
The heart of respect shall truly, become necessary.

Respectfulness,
Politeness,
And dedication to obedience,
Shall shield you from unnecessary troubles.

It should be known how truly outstanding a way of life the way of respect is, even just for getting on in this world. Therefore, the heart of respect is the first condition for entering the royal road. I wish to give a clear understanding of this condition, so let me give you some examples of people who took the opposite road. There was Nobunaga Oda, who was a Japanese warrior and feudal lord whose exceptional leadership could be recognized by anyone. But the way he died bespeaks something; what could it mean? It shows that in his life, he went down the path of might is right. The way his life ended shows us that he lacked the heart of respect.

Another example is the First Emperor of Qin (Qin Shi Huang), who, through his exceptional leadership ability, successfully combined all the lands of China into one. To these vast lands and its people, he was the first to bring unification, set up a central government, and found a nation based on the rule of law. There's no concealing this great accomplishment. But why did his life end in such tragedy? And why, only ten years after his death, did the Qin Dynasty collapse into obscurity? The reason was the merciless violence he used against a great number of people under the rule of law, the many philosophical books he burned, and the more than four hundred Confucian scholars he buried. By such acts as these, he treated people of excellence, who were devoted to conveying the heart of God and Heaven, as if they weren't even human. These are the acts that lack a heart of respect.

Rule by fear may seem to work for a time, but never in history has this form of rule lasted long. Rulers who govern people with fear will face a severe reaction and a miserable death. Therefore, my philosophy of the royal road differs from the "might is right" philosophy developed in the Middle Ages of Europe by Machiavelli and the use of trickery in Machiavellianism. His philosophy teaches the rule of might, which is a way of thinking that I do not take. Instead we need to firstly begin by entering the royal road.

3

WISDOM, THE SECOND CONDITION OF A TRUE LEADER

I have explained that the first condition of leadership is the heart of respect. So, what would the second condition be? I would like to say that this is wisdom. Wisdom is not knowledge alone, but results from knowledge transformed by experience. Having wisdom is a very vital condition of leadership, not just in the sense of being highly knowledgeable, but also in having a deep understanding of the human heart and mind and the ability to perceive others deeply, discern subtle human emotions, and sense subtle details. Wisdom as a virtue should have these qualities.

Because leaders must lead and nurture the many who follow them, they definitely need knowledge, experience, and what could be called profound wisdom that are exceeding those of the common people on this path. Said another way, leaders need the ability to understand others. People with a poor understanding of others lack a condition of leadership.

In these modern times, many people excelling at wisdom are becoming leaders in a variety of fields. In the highly information-reliant society of today, wisdom has played an extremely large role. So those who lack wisdom but hold leadership positions will need to have a competent assistant. Without one, it will be nearly impossible to rise to a position of leadership.

When we look at wisdom from another angle, we see that it also refers to a rare kind of creative power—the power to come up with new ideas one after another and accomplish creative work. This is an indispensable power for riding out times of confusion.

4

BELIEF, THE THIRD CONDITION OF A TRUE LEADER

The third condition for entering the royal road is belief. Basically, the base of this belief is faith in God, but the belief that leaders need is not limited to that. There are two other aspects of belief. The first is trust in other people—our friends, our many fellow compatriots. This aspect is indispensable to creating teamwork and collaborating on numerous tasks as an organization. But besides a belief in God and in friends or compatriots, the aspect of belief that is most important for a leader is trust from others—the feeling the leader inspires in others that makes them think, "I can believe in this person."

I wonder how many of my readers think about belief in this sense. Are you someone that others are able to believe in? Do your superiors, colleagues, family members, and subordinates regard you as someone to rely on? When others feel you deserve their trust, they should get inspired to stake something on you. A deceased prime minister of Japan once said, "Without the trust of the people there can be no government." How true these words are. Neither having a splendid career history nor any talents would enable a politician to serve as an able prime minister without the people's trust. When the people's trust in a leader wavers, his or her leadership cannot but dissolve away. This is something we've seen in recent events in which the loss of people's trust has led to politicians' downfall and removal from office.

Without the trust of the people there can be no government. How vital it is to be believed in by others. When you are a country's leader, the people's belief in you, their sense of confidence in you, is the reason they entrust you with the fate of their country. This is the reason that heads of state are given power over the lives and deaths of their people as their representatives.

When an untrusted leader takes hold of a leadership position, rule by terror arises straightaway, giving rise to a government that conceals the truth from the people and strives only to serve the government's own interests. People who do not follow the government are executed one after another—these are the kinds of circumstances that begin to arise. I want you to know how greatly vital it is for a leader to be held in trust. Please reflect upon and examine yourself in this respect. Think, how many people place their trust in you? How many people do you know who will tell you, "I believe in you one hundred percent," "If that's what you say, I believe you," or "If this is your decision, then I'll trust that it's the right thing to do."

You need many foundational elements to build people's trust. You may remember me saying that faith in God is the starting point; God gives those near Him attributes that serve as these foundational elements. What could these attributes be? One of them is a spirit of fairness and selflessness—a sense of fairness combined with a sense of selflessness. With this spirit, we seek to gain only a little for ourselves while treating others fairly. Another attribute is a lack of secretiveness, a capacity to live with openness and fairness. And also, no other attribute proves true leadership more eloquently than a history of bringing happiness to numerous people. As human beings born into this world, we find it hard to gain the trust of many people. Many of my readers may now realize how much of the conditions of leadership they have yet to attain.

5

RIGHTEOUSNESS, THE FOURTH CONDITION OF A TRUE LEADER

The first condition of leadership was respect, the second was wisdom, and the third was belief. The fourth important condition is righteousness. There are two aspects of the sense of righteousness. The first is the gratitude we feel for others; we feel grateful to people who have given us help, and we strive to repay them. We feel that we'll never forget the kindness we've received, and we want to return it to others someday. But this aspect of righteousness is not one of the conditions of leadership; it is rather an attribute of those who follow the leader.

It is the second aspect of righteousness that those who will be leaders possess. This is the ability to distinguish right from wrong—to understand the difference between right and wrong or good and evil. It is the power to determine what should be deemed right and what should be deemed wrong, the ability to separate the good from the bad. Said differently, this aspect of righteousness can be called sound judgment, the ability to perceive the soundness behind things. Put more simply, it is the ability to make decisions. This ability to discriminate the good from the evil, the right from the wrong, is a virtue that is indispensable to leaders or, at the very least, to those entering the royal path of the leader.

Some leaders live on the path of "might is right" and are expert at distinguishing not between right and wrong, but between what will serve their self-interests and what won't. This ability to judge what will be self-serving from what won't be doesn't accord with the sense of righteousness I have just described.

To be a true leader, you must have the power to see what's right and what's wrong. Some may wonder how this ability differs from wisdom—after all, if wisdom is the power of knowing things, then doesn't wisdom make this aspect of righteousness unnecessary? But you will see, even in your own experience, that there are many intelligent, learned, and knowledgeable people in the world who are unable to make decisions. They possess a lot of information and knowledge and are well-learned and well-educated, yet they are unable to make a judgment when a decision is most needed. Being stuck in indecisiveness, they are unable to judge between right and wrong, what to do and what not to do. As a matter of fact, the more their knowledge deepens and they learn about various things, the more complicated making decisions may become for them, and their ability to discern and discriminate grows ever weaker. Their accumulated knowledge becomes so great, they begin to overthink and lose sight of what is right and the choices that should be made. This is something that happens to people. In situations like this, we need to put our sense of righteousness to use, the righteousness we receive from God. We need to possess a definite sense of knowing what decision God earnestly wishes us to make.

Those in possession of this definite sense of where God's wishes lie may be struck, for a time, by surrounding circumstances that seem the very opposite of making progress, that seem like regress in terms of their own interests. When you have a strong sense of right and wrong and good and evil, you may be confronted, for a time, by a backwards course or a setback. But it is ultimately this heart of righteousness within you that will lead a great many people to have confidence in you. People ultimately gather to those who keep on choosing the good.

Leaders need to be supported by many people. A sense of righteousness, therefore, is a very important power to possess. However properly respectful you are, however knowledgeable you are, however abundant your wisdom is, and however great is the confidence others feel in you, a weakened sense of righteousness risks your decisions wavering in critical moments, bringing misery to a great number of people, and leading many of your people to their deaths in battle. It is of great necessity to possess the ability to make judgments and decisions.

6

COURAGE, THE FIFTH CONDITION OF A TRUE LEADER

The fifth condition of leadership is courage. Oh, how numerous the people are in these times who live without courage. Even when they look into their heart and recognize what is righteous and will benefit many people, oh, how so very many of them will not take action.

Finding so many people who lack courage is not a distress of mine alone. Many other thoughtful minds have shed tears at its stark absence among people who lack the courage to take action and take steps. However, let us not expect courage from the common people. Instead, of utmost importance now is for this virtue called courage to be imbued into each and every one of you who ought to become leaders. Even if you possess the righteousness to discern and judge right from wrong, how much could you ever accomplish without courageous action and steps? How much work could possibly be left behind on this Earth, if people were to cloister themselves in the mountains and say, "This is right," or "This is wrong," as if they have the ability to make judgments clairvoyantly? They'll leave behind but little to benefit others, because they lack the ability to act on their judgments and courage, even if they possessed such judiciousness.

When you do not have the power to take steps or carry things out decisively, people cannot but hesitate to recognize you as a leader. This holds true for our missionary activities in Happy Science. Unfortunately, people cannot qualify to be a leader, however outstanding the wisdom and level of study, if they are unable to guide even one person to the Truths. They won't measure up as a leader, unfortunately, if they cannot courageously take action, even if they do exceptionally well in their studies. This is something I would like to say.

7

SELF-REFLECTION ON THE FIVE VIRTUES OF LEADERSHIP

I have now set forth the five virtues, which are respect, wisdom, belief, righteousness, and courage. Based on these five virtues, please assess yourself one more time. First, are you practicing the attitude of respect? Have you ever been regarded as uncouth? Have you been crude in your behavior? Have you done anything to be embarrassed of if discovered by others— something that you've been concealing? You cannot enter the royal road if you have not fulfilled these points to begin with.

Next, there is the virtue of wisdom. How much have you studied, gained experience, and distilled lessons from your experience? These are the very questions you must ask yourself. It is impossible to lead others without something of value to convey to them. In any world you belong to, those to be leaders should possess something to pass down to other people. And we gain this something to convey through the very power of our wisdom. If, when you look within your heart, you find nothing of value to convey to others, it's undeniably an unfavorable sign of your capacity to be a leader.

There is also others' belief in you. There has never been a lasting period of rule by a ruler who has not earned the trust of his or her people. Among these false leaders were some who practiced various strategies to manipulate their own people out of distrustful feelings toward them. This approach may have seemed successful for a time, but in the final outcome, these leaders have found themselves alone and unaided. One cannot become a leader without others' trust.

Then there is a sense of righteousness. The ability to make judgments is the greatest weakness in some women. Some women still have only a frail ability to discern between good and evil or make immediate judgments about what to do and what not to do. But women who have a high capacity for leadership are highly capable of making decisions. Some are capable of reaching an answer immediately regarding what must be done, what shouldn't be done, and what is all right to do. Women who are able to do this have an extremely high capacity for leadership. But it is unfortunate to see a large number of women who are indecisive and go in circles because they are unable to make decisions.

Finally, there is courage. Righteousness must be followed by courage, which is the ability to take action and take steps. There are some people, whether male or female, with an exceptional ability to take steps. Some women in possession of this ability will, at times, live vigorously through their times to accomplish a great feat, surpassing even men. We mustn't forget that the courage of women has, in a sense, enough power to inspire the courage of all men.

8

Love, the Foundation of All Five Virtues

Ihave now discussed the five virtues. Yet even when you practice these five virtues and enter the royal road, there is still something missing that is necessary, and this something is the virtue lying at the foundation of all five virtues, underlying and supporting them. This is the principle of love, the same principle I've been teaching for many years at Happy Science. The power of love or, in other words, benevolence, is a necessary basis for these five virtues.

The heart of respect should have love. A heart of love should be at the basis of your giving of respect, your being respectful. However much you devote yourself to the practice of respectfulness, it cannot take root if it's aimed at your self-interest or self-gain.

You must also shape your wisdom through the heart of love. Your wisdom should be devoted to loving others and for the very purpose of bringing them greater happiness. There is no use for the kind of wisdom that is used to injure others. You must build your wisdom through love.

Then you must build people's belief in you and earn their confidence with your heart of love. You should not use others' belief in you to further your own self-interests or ambitions. We are not seeking a belief that's only skin-deep. We don't gain other people's trust through honeyed words, trying to win their favor, or appealing to their self-interests. You must act on your belief through the heart of love. And you must gather others' trust to yourself because of your love for them.

Furthermore, you must take righteous actions with love. Distinguish the good from the evil based on the heart of love; with love, discern where sound judgment lies; and make your decisions with a heart of love. Do not become a cold-hearted person as you do these things. People who are rational and logical cannot help but become cold-hearted at times. So you must always be conscious of acting righteously based on love.

Acts of courage must also have the heart of love. Acts of courage should not be based on recklessness. Courage is not to be used just to commit dangerous acts or bring you excitement. Courage should not just be sensational. Neither is courage to be used simply to get attention. Instead, you are to be someone whose love stirs you to act courageously. Because of your love for many others, you must stake your own life in vigorous acts of courage. You must not be mistaken in regard to these things. Acts of courage that do not arise from the heart of love are apt to become ambitious desires. Many among you may think you are acting with courage, but you are actually immersed in such desires. These include, for example, the heart that seeks self-gain—the heart that tries to obtain others' love. If this is the case with you, to act courageously you will need to cast out ambitious desires. And to cast out ambitious desires, you will need to practice a truly unconditional love for others. This is what "love that gives" means. This is the meaning of unconditional and selfless love. This is what "love that keeps giving" means. You absolutely must not use courageous action to serve your fame or to make a name for yourself in the world. Doing so will not keep you on the true royal road; instead it will be a trap leading you to the path of might is right.

9

ON THE ROYAL ROAD OF LIFE

I have explained how essential it is to practice the five merits with the heart of love. So when you put into practice these five paths of respectfulness, wisdom, belief, righteousness, and courage, what will manifest as a result? The five paths will manifest in you as moral excellence. They will become evident as virtue.

When people think about virtue, they usually think that it depends on how large or small their innate capacity is. But the inborn level of their capacity, the light within them, and the original level of Heaven they came from are actually associated with talents which cannot be changed through their own efforts. Contrary to this, virtue is something we can acquire and develop through our own efforts. As you practice the five kinds of virtues with the heart of love, you'll begin to shine as a true leader, leading to your gaining virtuousness. This path of becoming a true leader is the process of developing your virtues.

Where do you think virtuous people are? Yes, the royal road is where you'll find them. Gaining true mastery of the five virtues through practice is a tremendously arduous path to walk. Although you may be exceptional in one of them, there is almost always one or a few of them that you will find yourself deficient in. You may excel in respectfulness and wisdom but be lacking in your sense of righteousness and courage. You may have mastered belief, respectfulness, righteousness, and courage, but your wisdom may be insufficient. It is a certainty that there is an unevenness to our souls. But unless we can consciously see that we have developed at least three of the five virtues to an extraordinary level, we need to admit that we are a long way from entering the path of a true leader. At least three of them are necessary, and the remaining ones can be cultivated steadily through diligent effort. So if you realize where you are lacking, strive to fill in that area. This is how we grow toward human completion, and it's a very important thing we must do.

There is a reason why everyone finds themselves lacking in some of these virtues, and it is actually because of an astonishing truth. For example, based on the spiritual perspective that we believe in at Happy Science, the first condition, respectfulness, is a manifestation of the purple-colored light* representing obedience. The second condition, the virtue of wisdom, represents the golden-colored light of the spiritual Laws. There is also the blue-colored light of rational thinking, which also

---

* In the ninth-dimensional world of Heaven, God's light is divided into seven colors that flow down to the eighth-dimensional world of Heaven where it further separates into more than ten different colors. See Ryuho Okawa, *The Nine Dimensions* (New York: IRH Press, 2012).

manifests in the virtue of wisdom. Next, the virtue of belief is strongly manifested as the white-colored light of love. And there is also a sense of righteousness, the ability to discriminate the good from the bad, discern good from the evil, and distinguish where sound judgment lies. Finally, there is the virtue of courage, which is said to represent the red-colored light of justice. In this way, each virtue—respectfulness, wisdom, belief, righteousness, and courage—expresses one of the virtues of God. You will probably understand now the tremendous difficulty of attaining all five virtues. Certainly, you all possess strengths in some of these virtues. Somewhere among them, there should be ones in which you have been exceptional. But to truly reach completion as a human being, the tireless cultivation of all five paths is essential. This is the very course everyone will have to take to grow into a true leader like no other.

Many of the people who come to Happy Science and deeply study the Truths have come from at least the sixth-dimensional world of light in Heaven. Even the others who have not come from that world but are earnestly learning the Truths in this life, will, in my estimation, return to the sixth-dimensional world or beyond. Awaiting you there is the path to becoming a bodhisattva or a tathagata in the levels that are found further above.

This is a path that cannot be avoided, for God so commands it. When God brought human souls into creation and imbued each soul with individual character, He did so with this wish for us: "Become like me." Our individual human souls came into being as He said, "Become as I am." This being the case, our mission as human beings must be to answer this call that God gave us in the distant past, more than hundreds of millions or even billions of years ago. Therefore, there can be no other path for us, as human beings, but the royal road of life—the path to becoming true leaders of virtue by practicing the five virtues. Let us never give up walking, fall off, or recoil from this path. It is not a path for this life only. It is the path to walk, no matter how many times we are reborn.

CHAPTER SEVEN

THE AGE
OF
DAYBREAK

A SPECIAL LECTURE AT
THE UNIVERSITY OF TOKYO

1

FROM TAKING LOVE FROM OTHERS TO GIVING LOVE

I have heard it said about Zenjiro Yasuda, the benefactor of the Yasuda Auditorium at the University of Tokyo, that all through his life, he always had a certain phrase engraved in his heart. This phrase was "Cultivate the roots." I definitely notice the deep meaning of this phrase. A tree can be of any variety, but for it to grow, it needs to grow its roots deep and wide under the ground. For you to survive and grow even during times of change, you need to have grown your roots deeply under the ground. And this is true both for individual people and for all kinds of organizations, such as companies.

The most important thing for a college student to do is cultivate your roots. Time is very brief and flies by very quickly in college, so if you take your time, your college life will be over before you grow your roots into the ground and spread them out widely. It was over ten years ago that I, too, was a student at the University of Tokyo, and there are certain things I think you should bear in mind as a college student. So this is what I would like to talk about while I reflect on the experiences I had here.

From primary school until college, my fellow students had gotten all kinds of praise from their family, friends, and teachers. So they were apt to expect the praise of others as they went through their lives. This probably can't be helped, to a certain degree. But what might happen to you if receiving praise became the only purpose until the end of your life? I think that you would end up spending a long period of time, perhaps many decades, constantly taking love from numerous other people.

You will receive plenty of praise just from entering and graduating from this university; your entire lifetime shouldn't be spent seeking praise. Since you have gained many people's love and praise already, I think it is all the more important that you shift your mind from receiving to giving. Otherwise, what will become of the tax money your university received to attract exceptional students, provide exceptional educators in its faculty, and then send its students out into the world? It wouldn't be right at all if you only think about your self-interests.

In an old dormitory song of the forerunner to the University of Tokyo's Faculty of Liberal Arts, there is a line that says that when you stand up for something, nothing is impossible. I think these words are so true. But it seems that people here have forgotten this spirit. No graduates of the University of Tokyo have put their desperate efforts into serving others and the world for a long time. For example, the university was founded more than a century ago, but according to the mass media, I was the first of its graduates to found a religious organization. I am also the first former student of the Faculty of Law to become a religious leader. I am not saying this to boast. I am trying to say that for more than a century, graduates of this university have not become a religious leader. Why has this happened? Because the family members, friends, and peers of the students of this university did not value saving the people of this world and bringing them happiness. So these students chose other paths that would gain them recognition as exceptional people. Even now, as the students' graduation days near, they will choose highly esteemed paths according to society's values or other people's opinions and estimations. But I feel this is something to lament. Our aspirations should be much more about using our talents for the sake of as many people as possible. I want to ask you, without those aspirations, can you really call that a great achievement?

Please engrave deep into the folds of your heart at least a fragment of the words I say. I feel that because we live in times like ours today, it's all the more important for students to take adverse paths that never receive recognition. It is in these worlds where the spotlight has never shone that students can find new horizons where they can shine. How could you say you have real capabilities without becoming a pioneer there? If you have confidence in your capability, you should prove it in areas other people have avoided. Isn't it good for you to have times to discipline yourself through adversity? I think it is.

2

CULTIVATE YOUR ROOTS

The Path to Becoming a Cultivated Person

That is an important resolution and determination to hold of course, but to make your journey through life under that kind of resolution, you will need some kind of an asset as a foundation. What I mentioned earlier about cultivating your roots corresponds to this.

So, what kinds of efforts should you make to cultivate your roots? If you are a student, your efforts will be in the main area of your endeavors, which is your studies at school. While you are a university student, your main job is to study diligently in accordance with the school curriculum. This is a matter of course, but I think that even this is not quite enough. Graduates of the University of Tokyo regard themselves as members of the intelligentsia, and others regard them this way, too. But I think that even after you have made it through the university's curriculum, you are still going to be very far from the path of a true intellectual or a truly cultivated person. If you want to have confidence as a truly cultivated person, you will need to study a lot of things by yourself outside of university courses. Since each person's innate talent and accumulated effort are different, I cannot make a sweeping generalization, but reading at least a thousand excellent books is a first step to being admitted as a cultivated person.

Of course, it is easy for me to simply tell you that you should read a thousand books, but your college years are filled with all kinds of things to do, and time must seem to fly by. I still wish to tell you this, though. To develop your own ideas and present your own opinions, you need to read at least a thousand books on a wide variety of subjects. Without this level of reading as a basis, you will become an intellectual who is only able to restate things that others have already said. So you will need to reach that minimum level. If you cannot read this amount before your graduation, you should be able to do so in the course of a few additional years of effort afterward.

I do want to tell you, though, that even if you finish deeply reading a thousand books by the end of your four years at university, this will not get you any additional A's on your report card. Your time during these years will be limited, and students who invest this time in practical and goal-oriented ways will achieve high grades in their courses. To get good grades in your courses, you don't have to read a single book outside of your required reading lists, and you can focus completely on thoroughly studying your textbooks and going to your classes. In this sense, you won't receive any recognition for reading additional books; they won't make a difference in your grades or your diploma. But that only applies to the years before your graduation. Once you have graduated and entered the real world, whether you work in a company or at another kind of job, in five years' time, the students who have taken the path of cultivation that I've just described will see a clear difference between themselves and others. It is that they will be able to read people's minds and discern the true nature of the world, and as a result, they will be able to teach others.

The Path to Becoming a Thinker

I have just discussed the general path of becoming a cultivated person. What I would like to talk about next is the path for people who want to develop their own philosophy and establish themselves in the world as thinkers. There is no such thing as a formal path to becoming a thinker, so you have to blaze your own trail with your own efforts.

To give you simple criteria for that, you will need to read a minimum of two thousand books in order to make a profession from your opinions and philosophy. This is the very minimum level of reading you must do. If your intellectual life fails to reach this level, you will end up producing low-quality writing for hire. Two thousand books is the minimum level of reading you will need to form unique ideas and develop originality.

For example, if you were to read a hundred books every year, it would take you twenty years to read two thousand books. If you began at the age of twenty, you would be forty when you finished reading them all. So you can see why successful opinion leaders are typically, at youngest, in their forties, and most are in their fifties or sixties. It normally takes at least twenty years to accumulate the necessary level of knowledge.

If you want to enter the world of philosophy and influence people more quickly, you must accelerate this twenty- to thirty-year-long process. You will have to constantly do things in advance and reduce the time it takes. If you reduce it from twenty years down to ten, you will be able to enter this world a decade sooner. And you can shrink this period even further to enter this world even earlier. I, myself, am evidence of this process.

It's not easy to blaze your own trail, but if you continue to accumulate your store of knowledge, it will eventually reach a tipping point. When it does, you will experience great leaps, and your knowledge will transform into something completely different. To reach this point, the least amount of knowledge you will need is what you will find in one to two thousand books, as I have just described.

By contrast, the kind of intelligence that will help you get good grades in your classes is the kind that enables you to understand the rules for solving given problems or answering given questions. This doesn't require any creativity. This kind of intelligence has even been described as "slave intelligence."

At the same time, you don't gain creative intelligence just through any kind of inspiration or intuition. To receive inspirations and intuitions, you need to tirelessly cultivate a foundation of capability. The more you have cultivated this capability, the more extraordinary your ideas and intuitions will be.

Without knowledge of the already existing ideas that your predecessors have established, the ideas you come up with will have little originality. Carefully study works by predecessors from ancient times and others who have existed since then. Study the works that already exist, and select from among them the ideas you find most valuable. By accumulating one, two, three, or four extraordinary ideas that you agree with, you will steadily build an abundant store of knowledge. It's not until you create this minimum asset that you'll attain originality, and from that you will get completely new ideas no one has come up with before. Moreover, the ideas you develop will serve as guidance for people of later generations. So please understand that to establish original ideas and put them out into the world, you need to invest a great deal of time and effort.

3

THINK STRATEGICALLY

As you study in this way, you may find you don't get good results if you spend your time studying aimlessly, without any clear plan. So I would like to talk about this also. You shouldn't expect to reach your destination simply by accumulating time in study. Instead, you'll need to find the way to reap the greatest results from the one or two years you'll be investing in studying. You shouldn't invest this time aimlessly. Whether you spend one or two years studying, you have to base your approach on strategic thinking, so that you can reap the greatest results from your time.

What would strategic thinking be for a case such as this? You can divide it into several steps. The first step is to very clearly envision your objective, your destination. This step is extremely important. You need to begin with a clear sense of your goal, clearly seeing where you wish to be one year down the line, two years down the line, five years later, or ten years later. It's by taking this step and tracing backwards from your goal that you will see what you must do at this point, now. Unfortunately, this step of strategic thinking is difficult for many people to do during their college years. This is something that people often learn to do the hard way, as they gain experience out in society. Many people from provincial areas especially may lack strategic thinking, and unless they trace backwards from a very clear goal and set up a plan in this way, they will reap very little result for each unit of their time.

After you've set a clear goal, you will need to come up with a very clear method for allocating your time. Instead of always studying the same thing haphazardly, you should work on a variety of things simultaneously. This is the very method that will allow you to reap the greatest results per unit of your time. So please work on various subjects simultaneously. The same idea holds true in your academic endeavors. After you have identified what your goals are in each area of study, you will of course need to finish the courses in your main field of study within several years. But the other fields of study will take you far more time than that, perhaps five or ten years. So determine the point you want to have reached in each area of study five or ten years down the line, set these targets as your goals, and begin studying to reach them while you are in college. If you prepare for where you want to be not merely five or ten years later, but even twenty or thirty years later, over the course of five, ten, or twenty years, something will gradually blossom, even if your studies didn't bear any fruit while you were in college.

This is an important way of thinking. Strategic thinking wouldn't have that name if it resulted in immediate outcomes.

You may have goals for the immediate future, but the greatest journey is the path you'll start down now by sowing seeds that will bear fruit in one or two decades.

Moreover, very busy days are awaiting you when you enter the real world, so you'll make rather slow progress with your studies. Even the slightest interests and hobbies you dabbled in while in college can give you a helpful foothold for the future. This is why it's very important to widen your areas of interest and curiosity while you're still a student. There is no need for you to be successful in every area immediately. It is certain that you are not likely to succeed in the areas of interest you didn't cultivate while in college, even after five, ten, or twenty years since you entered the real world. This is why it is extremely important to diversify and expand your areas of interest now so you can sow these seeds for your future.

4
TAKE CARE OF YOURSELF PHYSICALLY

Another piece of advice is one that people rarely give you in college, and this is that your physical strength is extremely important. Students are young, and most of you have confidence in your physical strength, but when you graduate and gain experience in society, you'll begin to take less care of yourself physically. Then, no matter how much work you do, whether in your job or in some other endeavor, you won't be able to generate enough results. When your physical strength declines, it has a big effect on your intellectual life. This is why many people's intelligence suffers after college. They forget that being less careful about themselves physically can also affect their intellect.

That's why it's necessary to care for your physical condition appropriately. In addition, doing nothing but studying hard all the time can hinder your results. So, to increase your harvest, you need to do something different to refresh your mind. There are far too many people who don't realize that this is something they need to do. It's not good to always work yourself to the core. Doing physical activity or setting your work aside at intervals are the ways to reap greater results. Therefore, after you have studied for a period of time, try setting that subject aside for an interval of time to do something different, and then go back to that subject later.

When you study too hard in college, your energy and physical strength are depleted for a while after graduation, so it will take you a lot of time to recover from that. So when you're studying in college, please take care of yourself physically and give yourself intervals of time to do something else to refresh yourself. Please find some way to do that. It's very difficult to raise a sunken ship. Likewise, if you study too intently all the time, whether for two years or four years, you'll need a great deal of strength afterward to get your energy back. Please be very careful about this point.

5

Signs of a New Era

So far, I have been talking mainly about mindsets for college students. Next, I want to move on to the next subject. Can you comprehend these times we are living in now? We are now standing in the first half of the 1990s. Do you understand the meaning of these times?

The end of the century has come, and many forecasts are being debated. Will the coming years bring peace and stability, or will they bring conflict? The different views of future society are split into these two perspectives. But nothing has proved either of them, and many kinds of debates are happening everywhere. That's our current situation. But my view is that since the Gulf War occurred, the world definitely hasn't been heading toward peace and stability.

From this point on, the world will shift. You have surely heard about the pendulum effect. A pendulum that sways all the way to the right will always sway back to the left. That's also a law of history. When the times have swayed to one side, they've always then turned around to sway to the other side.

This age of peace and stability has already turned course toward the other direction. We're entering into an era of many powers conflicting with each other. And this confusion and conflict won't come to an end within ten years; it will continue for twenty years, and, depending on the situation, it could last as many as thirty years.

This is not confusion just for the sake of confusion. In the past, the United States and the Soviet Union have led the world as two superpowers. As their roles as superpowers conclude and the countries following them begin activities of self-realization on their own, there will be a lot of confusion. This confusion isn't necessarily an evil; it's a phase of active growth for the coming new age. You are on the verge of changes for the new century, and as you watch these changes, you are witnessing history. From now on, exciting things will be happening for young people. Traditional values will die out, and new ones will appear. No one knows exactly what new values will sweep the world. But the principles, the people, and the countries that will be leading the coming new age are now in their infancy and are beginning to grow. They are sprouting now, in this age. The seeds already exist. In this age we live in, the kind of thinking, the countries, and the people that will become world leaders in the next decade or two are appearing in various places. You must notice right away these things to become a forerunner of the coming age.

6

THE ROOTS OF DEMOCRACY

So, what kind of thinking will you need for the coming age—this new age with Japan at the center? To find out, you must once again question the principles that you have valued and thought to be right in these several decades. When you reconsider the principles you were taught to believe, had no doubts about, and accepted, the seeds of the new age will sprout from there.

For example, the system of democracy has faced little criticism. For more than forty years, the people of Japan have considered democracy to be national policy and have never opened it to criticism. It was believed to be good and was never questioned. But please think very carefully about this. The democracy that the Japanese people were taught to believe, that they accepted and spread without question throughout Japan is, in reality, a very formal and superficial interpretation.

The United States is a superpower of democracy. It is a country where democracy and capitalism have been combined, and experienced the greatest prosperity. The roots of American democracy originated with the English Puritans who sailed on the Mayflower. They founded America with a burning sense of mission as children of God and a wish to create a new, ideal world, while not forgetting the spirit of self-help. In this way, a splendid country was born, where Abraham Lincoln, who'd been born in a log cabin, could be accepted as a leader. Of course, it's now commonly known that the United States is approaching a period of decline. But please don't forget that in that land where democracy flourished, a virtuous, spiritual, and moral foundation firmly existed from the start.

When we look further back to two thousand several hundred years ago in ancient Greece, what was democracy like then? In those days, there wasn't anyone in those democratic societies who denied God. This was an age when the temple at Delphi existed and divinity and democracy existed together. What was behind this society that made a democracy like this possible?

Democracy has a splendid aspect that allows each person's talents and energy to flourish. In other words, it is a system of prosperity that lets everything flourish to its fullest. What is this right direction? It should aim for the ultimate ideal, which is God's ideal.

It is a historical fact that democracy flourishes best when it aims to realize God's ideal and build a kingdom of God on this Earth. In the more than forty years since the last world war, we, the people of Japan, have forgotten about that. We are apt to think of democracy as an election-based system and to look at it as simply a system of majority rule. If we're denying God, denying the nobleness of politics, and instead just chasing numbers, then we've already begun to transition into the "mobocracy" of the terminal period of ancient Greece.

What causes a democracy to become a mobocracy? This change occurs when the people start to lose their ideals and begin looking out for their self-interests and personal profits. When this happens, democracy turns into an ugly form of rule by the mob. America is facing this danger already, and the same holds true in Japan. A governing system like this is far from a true democracy.

Democracy bears its greatest fruits when exceptional people combine their strengths and strive with an entrepreneurial spirit and ethics to create an ideal society. But when everyone begins chasing personal self-interest and the opinion of the majority is made the opinion of all, that's the very beginning of the rule by the mass, a forerunner that leads to totalitarian rule by a dictatorship. This is why every person in a democratic system needs to have awakened and be burning with ideals.

This is also a reason why I've discussed the importance of reading and studying. You can become influenced by superficial, skin-deep ways of thinking unless you've studied sufficiently and established your own thoughts and perspectives. You can see this happening here and there with various people's opinions already. If all citizens are induced by these types of opinions, we'll surely be led to a great downfall. The prospects will become very dark for everyone.

We need to go back to the original spirit of democracy and understand that growth should be based on the efforts and competition of people who've developed a virtuous foundation and a moral spirit. And we need to realize that democracy is definitely not incompatible with religion, even though the Japanese media has denied religion since after the last world war. We cannot make that mistake. In the mass media, some people see religion as an enemy of democracy, but that's just because they haven't studied the matter enough. If you look back at history, the seeds of democracy were already contained in the teachings of Jesus, who taught that we human beings are children of God. He said that your rank in society and whether or not you receive recognition in this world make no difference. Everyone's soul is a splendid child of God, and everyone is equal as a soul. What is good and right is when the soul repents, converts, and lives purely by giving love to others. It's when people do this that we recognize them as splendid people. Our jobs and social status make no difference to that at all. This was the thinking at the very starting point of democracy.

In the time of Jesus, those held in esteem were rabbis who taught others about the traditional teachings of Moses. Roman officials were also held in high regard. By contrast, the people who were disliked the most were the publicans—the tax collectors. The people who are most respected in our times in Japan, the people of the Ministry of Finance, were of the lowest social class in Jesus's time. In addition to that class, there were also prostitutes. Jesus was extremely kind to people of these classes, who faced a lot of discrimination. He also taught them about our equality as souls. He taught them that they, too, have a chance to enter Heaven and that even if you are underprivileged in the worldly sense, you can be saved by connecting with God. These teachings also became the origins of democracy.

We can also go back further, to five hundred years before Jesus's time—the time of Shakyamuni Buddha and his teachings. India had a caste system, and class discrimination at that time was extremely strong. Shakyamuni Buddha disputed the caste system with his philosophy.

Shakyamuni Buddha did away with this system in his order of disciples, the sangha. He taught his disciples that to receive recognition as an exceptional person, it makes no difference whether you come from the Brahman, Kshatriya, Vaishya, or Shudra class. Everyone carries a seed of Buddha within them. Everyone has buddha-nature. We human beings truly awaken and become splendid when we make our buddha-nature shine. We can become exceptional people when we make efforts and persevere with God's mind as our own mind. The social class you come from or your education as a brahman makes no difference.

When you search out the roots of democracy in this way, you will find a principle of salvation, a principle of courage for many people, and the greatest principle of prosperity. And anyone can experience this salvation and this prosperity if they are courageous and make the effort to grasp new opportunities. That was the origin of democracy. That was God's teaching of equality. Religion teaches that our souls originally shine like diamonds. Over the course of our many past incarnations, the capacity of our souls may have varied in size. We have different strengths and weaknesses. We may have different shapes. But no matter how many differences there are or how different our capacity or our brightness may be, everyone has the soul of a diamond. These are the things that religions have taught about. This is why we are taught to polish the diamond, the gem within us, according to our individual capacities and circumstances. This is the most fundamental equality among all individuals.

Furthermore, the efforts we make in this life to polish our souls will be measured using the yardstick of fairness. Everyone is equal from the beginning. On the other hand we are measured according to the direction of the efforts we've made and the fruits we've reaped from those efforts. This is another criteria called fairness. Our level of enlightenment, our capacity to guide others, and the spiritual grade in our afterlife are determined according to fairness.

In this way, God gave humankind two measuring sticks, equality and fairness, to facilitate our soul-training on Earth. God teaches that He uses these measuring sticks to measure all people, so we all must do our utmost to live the best lives we can on this Earth, and open the path to happiness.

7

The Age of the Sun

an you now see the shape of what happiness is? The happiness that I teach is a little different from the happiness of worldly achievements. My teachings instruct everyone to make the essence of their soul shine, and not only that, but also to shine that inner light out into the world. Those who have gained happiness in the true sense are the enlightened ones, and enlightened ones are capable of making many people in the world happy. In this sense, personal happiness can lead to public happiness. And when we look deeply at the path of soul-training, the path to each person's enlightenment, we can see the possibility of creating utopia on Earth.

The utopia that we at Happy Science seek first manifests in this way within the mind of each person and then is shined upon each of our countries and the world. I believe that you will find your future within this path to true happiness, within the true, splendid meaning of religion, which does away with the religions that have existed until now.

I have no doubt that the twenty-first century will become an age of religion. This movement has already begun. Needless to say, both in Japan and worldwide, a new religious century is about to begin. This is undoubtedly the trend of the coming age. At present, many students may go into fields of business, not that of religion. But in the twenty-first century, businesses also have to uphold ideas based on religious values that seek people's happiness. They will be the ones to grow.

Neither technical skills, publicity skills, renown, or the difficulty of getting in are what really matters. In the twenty-first century, what really matters are activities that have spiritual Truth-value. Please engrave that deeply into your heart. Young generations are living in the daybreak of their lives. Similarly, the world is also experiencing the age of daybreak, an era of refounding nations, an age of new genesis. In this Age of Daybreak, the sun of Truths will rise and the Age of the Sun will come to you all. In this Age of Daybreak, we must renew our resolve and make daily efforts so that we can realize the Age of the Sun, the Century of Happiness, the second founding, and the second creation of utopia on Earth.

Afterword

In publishing this newly released, revised edition of this book, I have added a new chapter, chapter 7, "The Age of Daybreak." It was a very hot day on May 26, 1991. In front of the Yasuda Auditorium on the University of Tokyo's Hongo Campus, a closely packed crowd of two thousand and several hundred people gathered mainly from the students of that university. It was my first public appearance, aside from our events at Happy Science, and also the first lecture I had ever given outdoors. Under bad acoustics and a blazing sun, I spoke for approximately one hour.

While I spoke, memories of my own student days a decade before crossed my mind many times, and I even sensed my own twenty-year-old eyes looking at me from the audience. There had been friendships. There had been loves. There had been days when I reduced my daily spending to five hundred yen so I could afford to buy books. There were days I dreamed of becoming a poet and days I thought I'd become a philosopher. There was also the day I received a telegram saying, "Father critically ill come home." As I held it in my hand, I made the decision to give up the path of academia and choose to be employed at a company to help support my family.

The days of my youth held joy, but more than that, they held sadness. With these bittersweet memories in my heart, I stood at the podium with the students' curious eyes looking up at me. There must have been an awakened one who'd just started the path of a strange destiny, one who is "crying in the wilderness."

The year 1991 was a time I was plunged into a fight for the Truths after that special lecture at the University of Tokyo. What began was a fated battle, a fight against an enemy of Truths. And that fight still continues.

A new religion must fight against prejudice, misunderstanding, malice, and even the devils themselves to take root in this world. Such toil is necessary to bring about the age of daybreak for humankind. This book of Truths is my gift to the youth of future generations.

Ryuho Okawa
President
Happy Science
March 1993

The contents of this book were compiled from the following lectures given by Ryuho Okawa.

Chapter One
"Introduction to the Royal Road of Life"
Morning of June 3, 1990
Makuhari Messe in Chiba prefecture
(Japanese Title: *Jinsei No Oudou Wo Kataru [Joron]*)

Chapter Two
"Serenity of Mind"
November 25, 1989
Ichinomiya Civic Hall in Aichi prefecture
(Japanese Title: *Heiseishin*)

Chapter Three
"Rebuilding Your Life"
May 20, 1990
Hiroshima Sun Plaza in Hiroshima prefecture
(Japanese Title: *Jinsei No Saiken*)

Chapter Four
"Living in Eternity Now"
July 29, 1990

Aichi Prefectural Gymnasium in Aichi prefecture

(Japanese Title: *Eien No Ima Wo Ikiru*)

Chapter Five
"The Path to Human Completion"
August 6, 1989

Sapporo Education and Culture Hall in Hokkaido

(Japanese Title: *Ningen Kansei E No Michi*)

Chapter Six
"On the Royal Road of Life"
Afternoon of June 3, 1990

Makuhari Messe in Chiba prefecture

(Japanese Title: *Jinsei No Oudou Wo Kataru*)

Chapter Seven
"The Age of Daybreak"
May 26, 1991

In front of the Yasuda Auditorium at the University of Tokyo in Tokyo

(Japanese Title: *Reimei No Jidai*)

ABOUT THE AUTHOR

Ryuho Okawa was born on July 7th 1956, in Tokushima prefecture, Japan. After graduating from the University of Tokyo with a law degree, he joined a Tokyo-based trading house. While working at its New York headquarters, he studied international finance at the Graduate Center of the City University of New York. In 1981, he attained Great Enlightenment and became aware that he is El Cantare with a mission to bring salvation to all of humankind. In 1986 he established Happy Science. It now has members in over 100 countries across the world, with more than 700 local branches and temples as well as 10,000 missionary houses around the world. The total number of lectures has exceeded 3,000 (of which more than 140 are in English) and over 2,600 books (of which more than 500 are Spiritual Interview Series) have been published, many of which are translated into 31 languages. Many of the books, including *The Laws of the Sun* have become best sellers or million sellers.

Up to date, Happy Science has produced 18 movies. These projects were all planned by the executive producer, Ryuho Okawa. Recent movie titles are *Life is Beautiful – Heart to Heart 2 –* (documentary released Aug. 2019), *Immortal Hero* (live-action movie to be released Oct. 2019), and *Shinrei Kissa EXTRA no Himitsu – The Real Exorcist –* (literally, "The Secret of Spirits' Café EXTRA – The Real Exorcist –," live-action movie in May 2020). He has also composed the lyrics and music of over 100 songs, such as theme songs and featured songs of movies. Moreover, he is the Founder of Happy Science University and Happy Science Academy (Junior and Senior High School), Founder and President of the Happiness Realization Party, Founder and Honorary Headmaster of Happy Science Institute of Government and Management, Founder of IRH Press Co., Ltd., and the Chairperson of New Star Production Co., Ltd. and ARI Production Co., Ltd.

WHAT IS EL CANTARE?

El Cantare means "the Light of the Earth," and is the
Supreme God of the Earth who has been guiding humankind
since the beginning of Genesis. He is whom Jesus called
Father, and His branch spirits, such as Shakyamuni Buddha
and Hermes, have descended to Earth many times and helped
to flourish many civilizations. To unite various religions and
to integrate various fields of study in order to build a new
civilization on Earth, a part of the core consciousness has
descended to Earth as Master Ryuho Okawa.

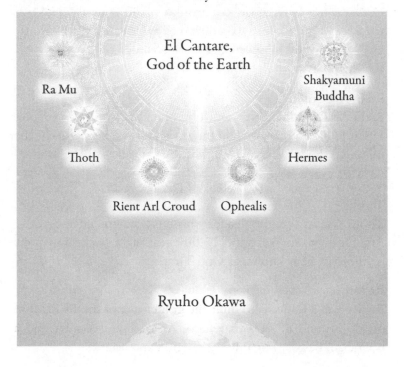

El Cantare,
God of the Earth

Ra Mu

Shakyamuni
Buddha

Thoth

Hermes

Rient Arl Croud   Ophealis

Ryuho Okawa

Shakyamuni Buddha
Gautama Siddhartha was born as a prince into the Shakya Clan in India around 2,600 years ago. When he was 29 years old, he renounced the world and sought enlightenment. He later attained Great Enlightenment and founded Buddhism.

Hermes
In the Greek mythology, Hermes is thought of as one of the 12 Olympian gods, but the spiritual Truth is that he taught the teachings of love and progress around 4,300 years ago that became the origin of the rise of the Western civilization. He is a hero that truly existed.

Ophealis
Ophealis was born in Greece around 6,500 years ago and was the leader who took an expedition to as far as Egypt. He is the God of miracles, prosperity, and arts, and is known as Osiris in the Egyptian mythology.

Rient Arl Croud
Rient Arl Croud was born as a king of the ancient Incan Empire around 7,000 years ago and taught about the mysteries of the mind. In the heavenly world, he is responsible for the interactions that take place between various planets.

Thoth
Thoth was an almighty leader who built the golden age of the Atlantic civilization around 12,000 years ago. In the Egyptian mythology, he is known as God Thoth.

Ra Mu
Ra Mu was a leader who built the golden age of the civilization of Mu around 17,000 years ago. As a religious leader and a politician, he ruled by uniting religion and politics.

ABOUT HAPPY SCIENCE

Happy Science is a global movement that empowers individuals to find purpose and spiritual happiness and to share that happiness with their families, societies, and the world. With more than twelve million members around the world, Happy Science aims to increase awareness of spiritual truths and expand our capacity for love, compassion, and joy so that together we can create the kind of world we all wish to live in.

Activities at Happy Science are based on the Principles of Happiness (Love, Wisdom, Self-Reflection, and Progress). These principles embrace worldwide philosophies and beliefs, transcending boundaries of culture and religions.

Love teaches us to give ourselves freely without expecting anything in return; it encompasses giving, nurturing, and forgiving.

Wisdom leads us to the insights of spiritual truths, and opens us to the true meaning of life and the will of God (the universe, the highest power, Buddha).

Self-Reflection brings a mindful, nonjudgmental lens to our thoughts and actions to help us find our truest selves—the essence of our souls—and deepen our connection to the highest power. It helps us attain a clean and peaceful mind and leads us to the right life path.

Progress emphasizes the positive, dynamic aspects of our spiritual growth—actions we can take to manifest and spread happiness around the world. It's a path that not only expands our soul growth, but also furthers the collective potential of the world we live in.

PROGRAMS AND EVENTS

The doors of Happy Science are open to all. We offer a variety of programs and events, including self-exploration and self-growth programs, spiritual seminars, meditation and contemplation sessions, study groups, and book events.

Our programs are designed to:
* Deepen your understanding of your purpose and meaning in life
* Improve your relationships and increase your capacity to love unconditionally
* Attain peace of mind, decrease anxiety and stress, and feel positive
* Gain deeper insights and a broader perspective on the world
* Learn how to overcome life's challenges
    ... and much more.

*For more information, visit **happy-science.org**.*

CONTACT INFORMATION

Happy Science is a worldwide organization with faith centers around the globe. For a comprehensive list of centers, visit the worldwide directory at *happy-science.org*. The following are some of the many Happy Science locations:

UNITED STATES AND CANADA

New York
79 Franklin St., New York, NY 10013
Phone: 212-343-7972
Fax: 212-343-7973
Email: ny@happy-science.org
Website: happyscience-na.org

New Jersey
725 River Rd, #102B, Edgewater, NJ 07020
Phone: 201-313-0127
Fax: 201-313-0120
Email: nj@happy-science.org
Website: happyscience-na.org

Florida
5208 8th St., St. Zephyrhills, FL 33542
Phone: 813-715-0000
Fax: 813-715-0010
Email: florida@happy-science.org
Website: happyscience-na.org

Atlanta
1874 Piedmont Ave., NE Suite 360-C
Atlanta, GA 30324
Phone: 404-892-7770
Email: atlanta@happy-science.org
Website: happyscience-na.org

San Francisco
525 Clinton St.
Redwood City, CA 94062
Phone & Fax: 650-363-2777
Email: sf@happy-science.org
Website: happyscience-na.org

Los Angeles
1590 E. Del Mar Blvd., Pasadena, CA 91106
Phone: 626-395-7775
Fax: 626-395-7776
Email: la@happy-science.org
Website: happyscience-na.org

Orange County
10231 Slater Ave., #204
Fountain Valley, CA 92708
Phone: 714-745-1140
Email: oc@happy-science.org
Website: happyscience-na.org

San Diego
7841 Balboa Ave., Suite #202
San Diego, CA 92111
Phone: 619-381-7615
Fax: 626-395-7776
E-mail: sandiego@happy-science.org
Website: happyscience-na.org

Hawaii
Phone: 808-591-9772
Fax: 808-591-9776
Email: hi@happy-science.org
Website: happyscience-na.org

Kauai
4504 Kukui Street Suite 207, Kappa,
HI 96746, U.S.A.
Phone: 808-822-7007
Fax: 808-822-6007
Email: kauai-hi@happy-science.org
Website: kauai.happyscience-na.org

Toronto

845 The Queensway
Etobicoke ON M8Z 1N6 Canada
Phone: 1-416-901-3747
Email: toronto@happy-science.org
Website: happy-science.ca

INTERNATIONAL

Tokyo

1-6-7 Togoshi, Shinagawa
Tokyo, 142-0041 Japan
Phone: 81-3-6384-5770
Fax: 81-3-6384-5776
Email: tokyo@happy-science.org
Website: happy-science.org

London

3 Margaret St.
London,W1W 8RE United Kingdom
Phone: 44-20-7323-9255
Fax: 44-20-7323-9344
Email: eu@happy-science.org
Website: happyscience-uk.org

Sydney

516 Pacific Hwy, Lane Cove North,
NSW 2066, Australia
Phone: 61-2-9411-2877
Fax: 61-2-9411-2822
Email: sydney@happy-science.org

Brazil Headquarters

Rua. Domingos de Morais 1154,
Vila Mariana, Sao Paulo
SP-CEP 04009-002, Brazil
Phone: 55-11-5088-3800
Fax: 55-11-5088-3806
Email: sp@happy-science.org
Website: happyscience.com.br

Jundiai

Rua Congo, 447, Jd. Bonfiglioli
Jundiai-CEP, 13207-340
Phone: 55-11-4587-5952
Email: jundiai@happy-science.org

Vancouver

#201-2607 East 49th Avenue
Vancouver, BC, V5S 1J9, Canada
Phone: 1-604-437-7735
Fax: 1-604-437-7764
Email: vancouver@happy-science.org
Website: happy-science.ca

Seoul

74, Sadang-ro 27-gil,
Dongjak-gu, Seoul, Korea
Phone: 82-2-3478-8777
Fax: 82-2-3478-9777
Email: korea@happy-science.org
Website: happyscience-korea.org

Taipei

No. 89, Lane 155, Dunhua N. Road
Songshan District, Taipei City 105, Taiwan
Phone: 886-2-2719-9377
Fax: 886-2-2719-5570
Email: taiwan@happy-science.org
Website: happyscience-tw.org

Malaysia

No 22A, Block 2, Jalil Link Jalan Jalil Jaya 2,
Bukit Jalil 57000, Kuala Lumpur, Malaysia
Phone: 60-3-8998-7877
Fax: 60-3-8998-7977
Email: malaysia@happy-science.org
Website: happyscience.org.my

Nepal

Kathmandu Metropolitan City Ward No.
15, Ring Road, Kimdol,
Sitapaila Kathmandu, Nepal
Phone: 97-714-272931
Email: nepal@happy-science.org

Uganda

Plot 877 Rubaga Road, Kampala
P.O. Box 34130, Kampala, Uganda
Phone: 256-79-3238-002
Email: uganda@happy-science.org
Website: happyscience-uganda.org

ABOUT IRH PRESS USA

IRH Press USA Inc. was founded in 2013 as an affiliated firm of IRH Press Co., Ltd. Based in New York, the press publishes books in various categories including spirituality, religion, and self-improvement and publishes books by Ryuho Okawa, the author of over 100 million books sold worldwide. For more information, visit *okawabooks.com*.

Follow us on:

Facebook: Okawa Books   **Twitter**: Okawa Books
Goodreads: Ryuho Okawa   **Instagram**: OkawaBooks
Pinterest: Okawa Books

RYUHO OKAWA'S LAWS SERIES

The Laws Series is an annual volume of books that are mainly comprised of Ryuho Okawa's lectures on various topics that highlight principles and guidelines for the activities of Happy Science every year. *The Laws of the Sun*, the first publication of the laws series, ranked in the annual best-selling list in Japan in 1994. Since then, all of the laws series' titles have ranked in the annual best-selling list for more than two decades, setting socio-cultural trends in Japan and around the world.

THE TRILOGY

The first three volumes of the Laws Series, *The Laws of the Sun*, *The Golden Laws*, and *The Nine Dimensions* make a trilogy that completes the basic framework of the teachings of God's Truths. *The Laws of the Sun* discusses the structure of God's Laws, *The Golden Laws* expounds on the doctrine of time, and *The Nine Dimensions* reveals the nature of space.

BOOKS BY RYUHO OKAWA

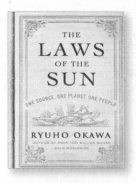

THE LAWS OF THE SUN

One Source, One Planet, One People

Paperback • 288 pages • $15.95
ISBN: 978-1-942125-43-3

In this powerful book, Ryuho Okawa reveals the transcendent nature of consciousness and the secrets of our multi-dimensional universe and our place in it. By understanding the different stages of love and following the Buddhist Eightfold Path, he believes we can speed up our eternal process of development. *The Laws of the Sun* shows the way to realize true happiness—a happiness that continues from this world through the other.

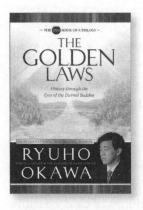

THE GOLDEN LAWS

History through the Eyes of the Eternal Buddha

Paperback • 216 pages • $14.95
ISBN: 978-1-941779-81-1

Throughout history, Great Guiding Spirits of Light have been present on Earth in both the East and the West at crucial points in human history to further our spiritual development. *The Golden Laws* reveals how a Divine Plan has been unfolding on Earth, and outlines thousands of years of the secret history of humankind. Once we understand the true course of history, through past, present, and into the future, we cannot help but become aware of the significance of our spiritual mission in the present age.

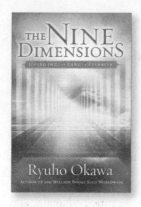

THE NINE DIMENSIONS

Unveiling the Laws of Eternity

Paperback • 168 pages • $15.95
ISBN: 978-0-982698-56-3

This book is a window into the mind of our loving God, who designed this world and the vast, wondrous world of our afterlife as a school with many levels through which our souls learn and grow. When the religions and cultures of the world discover the truth of their common spiritual origin, they will be inspired to accept their differences, come together under faith in God, and build an era of harmony and peaceful progress on Earth.

THE LAWS OF GREAT ENLIGHTENMENT

Always Walk with Buddha

Paperback • 232 pages • $17.95
ISBN: 978-1-942125-62-4

Constant self-blame for mistakes, setbacks, or failures and feelings of unforgivingness toward others are hard to overcome. Through the power of enlightenment we can learn to forgive ourselves and others, overcome life's problems, and courageously create a brighter future ourselves. *The Laws of Great Enlightenment* addresses the core problems of life that people often struggle with and offers advice on how to overcome them based on spiritual truths.

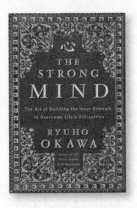

THE STRONG MIND

The Art of Building the Inner Strength
to Overcome Life's Difficulties

Paperback • 192 pages • $15.95
ISBN: 978-1-942125-36-5

In this book, Ryuho Okawa shares his
personal experiences as examples to show
how we can build toughness of the heart,
develop richness of the mind, and cultivate
the power of perseverance. The strong mind
is what we need to rise time and again, and
to move forward no matter what difficulties we face in life. This book
will inspire and empower you to take courage, develop a mature and
cultivated heart, and achieve resilience and hardiness so that you can
break through the barriers of your limits and keep winning in the battle
of your life.

THE CHALLENGE OF THE MIND

An Essential Guide to Buddha's Teachings:
Zen, Karma, and Enlightenment

Paperback • 208 pages • $16.95
ISBN: 978-1-942125-45-7

In this book, Ryuho Okawa explains
essential Buddhist tenets and how to put
these ideas into practice. Enlightenment
is not just an abstract idea but one that
everyone can experience to some extent.
In clear but thought-provoking language,
Okawa imbues new life into traditional teachings and offers a solid
basis of reason and intellectual understanding to often overcompli-
cated Buddhist concepts. By applying these basic principles to our
lives, we can direct our minds to higher ideals and create a bright
future for ourselves and others.

THE LAWS OF INVINCIBLE LEADERSHIP
An Empowering Guide for Continuous and
Lasting Success in Business and in Life

THE STARTING POINT OF HAPPINESS
An Inspiring Guide to Positive Living with Faith, Love, and Courage

INVINCIBLE THINKING
An Essential Guide for a Lifetime of Growth, Success, and Triumph

HEALING FROM WITHIN
Life-Changing Keys to Calm, Spiritual, and Healthy Living

THE UNHAPPINESS SYNDROME
28 Habits of Unhappy People (and How to Change Them)

THE LAWS OF SUCCESS
A Spiritual Guide to Turning Your Hopes Into Reality

THINK BIG!
Be Positive and Be Brave to Achieve Your Dreams

THE MOMENT OF TRUTH
Become a Living Angel Today

CHANGE YOUR LIFE, CHANGE THE WORLD
A Spiritual Guide to Living Now

*For a complete list of books, visit **okawabooks.com**.*